ZAMBIA BASIC EDUCATIO

ENVIRONMENTAL
SCIENCE

7

PUPILS' BOOK

LONGMAN

Longman Zimbabwe (Pvt) Ltd
Tourle Road, Ardbennie, Harare

Associated companies, branches and representatives
throughout the world

© Curriculum Development Centre, 1998

First published 1998

ISBN   9982 19 079 2

Text set in 12/14 Stone Serif

DTP by Matambudziko Dzikiti

Illustrated by A. Dhliwayo, T. Chodewa, H. Mussa

Cover design and illustration by Abel Dhliwayo

Printed by CTP, Cape Town

The publisher's policy is to use paper manufactured
from sustainable forests.

Contents

Acknowledgements

This book was revised in a series of writing workshops at the Curriculum Development Centre (CDC), in order to address concepts and new knowledge contained in the revised syllabus.

The Curriculum Development Centre acknowledges the contributions of the original authors for their tireless efforts and contributions on the first edition of the book. To this effect special thanks go to the following:

Mike Mackrory and the school teachers that participated in the first edition.

CDC also wishes to acknowledge the contributions and suggestions from the members of the revision team. In this respect special thanks go to the following:

A Chengo	S Hikaula	G Mutambo
J Shiyanda	E Nyambe	C Malilwe

Sincere gratitude goes to the institutions which allowed their members of staff to participate in this important exercise.

Finally, special thanks go to the Zambia Education Rehabilitation Project (ZERP) for providing the financial and material support during the preparation and revision of this course.

Curriculum Development Centre

Preface

This Environmental Science Course book has been prepared against the background of the Focus on Learning Document (1992) and of the Basic Education Syllabus (Grades 1 - 7).

The Ministry of Education, under the auspices of the Curriculum Development Centre (CDC), carried out a Primary Education Curriculum revision between August and November, 1993. During this exercise the Grades 1 - 7 syllabi were revised. After the revision exercise, the Grades 5 - 7 Teacher's and Pupils' Books were further revised in order to reflect closely the revised version of the syllabi in the course materials.

The revision of this course was carried out with funding from the Zambia Education Rehabilitation Project (ZERP). It is my sincere hope that learners and teachers will find this Environmental Science course useful.

M.E. Katengo
DIRECTOR
CURRICULUM DEVELOPMENT CENTRE

Chapter 1

ELECTRICITY

Conductors and insulators

Objective

By the end of this chapter you should be able to:
*   identify conductors and insulators.

Activities

1   In groups, make a simple circuit. Place a dry cell and a torch bulb into holders. Join one end of the dry cell to the bulb with a connecting wire. Join the other end of the dry cell to the paper clip/switch, with another connecting wire. Set up the diagram as shown below:

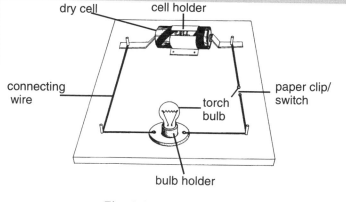

dry cell   cell holder

connecting wire

torch bulb

paper clip/ switch

bulb holder

Fig. 1.1.1 Simple circuit

2   Take another connecting wire. Connect one end of the wire to the bulb. Close the gap by touching the paper clips.
   [?]   What happens to the bulb?
   [?]   What causes this?

3   Replace the paper clip with one of the following materials: steel nail, piece of wood, iron nail, piece of rubber, pencil lead, piece of glass, aluminum foil, plastic comb, piece of paper.

❓ What happens to the bulb when you use one of the following? Record your observations in the table that follows.

Material	Observation
steel nail	
piece of wood	
iron nail	
piece of rubber	
piece of glass	
plastic comb	
piece of paper	
pencil lead	
aluminum foil	

Information

Materials through which electricity can flow are called **conductors**. Examples of conductors are **steel, silver, aluminum**, and **copper**. Generally **metals** are conductors of electricity. Materials which do not allow electricity to pass through them are called **insulators**. Examples of insulators are **rubber, paper, glass, cotton, dry air, wood** and **plastic**.

An **electric circuit** is a complete path through which electricity flows. The bulb lit up because electricity passed through conductors. When some materials were placed across the gap the bulb did not light up because they were insulators which do not allow electricity to flow through them.

✎ Written exercise 1.1

Fill in the blank spaces by using the following words:
cell, rubber, conductors, electric, silver, wood, iron, insulators

1 Materials which allow electricity to flow through them are called _____ .

2 Materials that do not allow electricity to pass through them are called _____ .

3 _____ , copper, _____ and aluminum are examples of conductors.

4 _____ , cotton, _____ and dry air are examples of insulators.

5 A complete pathway through which electricity flows is called an _____ circuit.

Activity Set 2

Series and parallel connections

Objective

By the end of this section you should be able to:
• demonstrate how to connect bulbs in series and in parallel.

Activities

Set up a simple electric circuit by doing the following:

1 Place two torch bulbs and a dry cell in holders as shown in the diagram below. Use connecting wires to connect the dry cell to the switch and to the torch bulbs. Connect the other end of the dry cell to the switch.

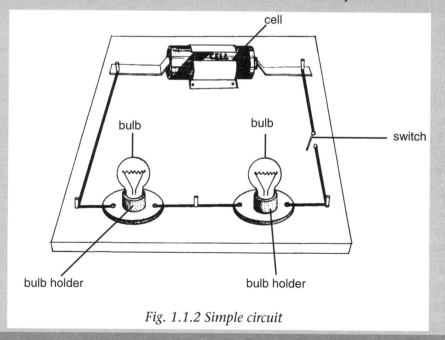

Fig. 1.1.2 Simple circuit

2 Close the switch and observe.
   ? What happens to the bulbs? Why?
3 Let the switch remain closed. Remove one of the two bulbs from the circuit.
   ? What happens to the bulb in the circuit? Why?
4 Rearrange the circuit as shown in the diagram below:

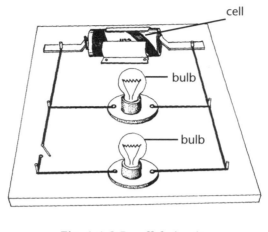

Fig. 1.1.3 Parallel circuit

5 Close the switch and observe.
   ? What happens to the bulbs? Why?
6 Let the switch remain closed. Remove one of the two bulbs from the circuit.
   ? What happens to the bulb in the circuit? Why?

Information

There are two ways to connect bulbs in an electric circuit. The electric circuit where the bulbs and a cell are joined together in one pathway is called a **series circuit**.

When one bulb is removed in the series circuit, the remaining bulb goes off.

The bulb in the circuit goes off because there is a break in the circuit created by the removed bulb.

The other way of connecting bulbs in an electric circuit is called a **parallel circuit**. In the parallel connection, parts, for example, the bulbs, have junctions where the pathway branches, or is divided.

In parallel connections, the removed bulb does not create a gap for the remaining bulb in the circuit. Parallel connections are used in domestic electric circuits. The use of parallel circuits in homes does not affect lighting in other bulbs when one or more bulbs are blown or have stopped working. The remaining bulbs in various rooms continue to give light.

Written exercise 1.2

Use words from the list to complete the sentences:
battery, bulbs, circuits, light, series, parallel, cells, symbol

1 In the ——————— connections, the bulbs and the ——————— are joined together in one pathway.
2 In the ———————connections, the ——————— and cells have junctions where the pathway divides or branches.
3 What do the symbols below represent?

Activity Set 3

Fuses, trip switches and wiring in plugs

Objectives

By the end of this section you should be able to:
*   describe wiring in a 13 amp plug.
*   describe the action of a fuse, a trip switch and their correct positions in a circuit.

Activities

1 Take the 13 amp 3 pin plug which does not have a cable connected to it. Use a screwdriver to remove the cover.
    ? How many pin heads are there?
    ? What letters are on each pin head?
    ? What do these letters stand for?
    ? What else can you see apart from the pin heads?
2 Take a 20 cm electric cable. Use a cutting blade or cable stripper to open the outer covering of the end of the electric cable. The diagram on page 6 shows the cable with 5 cm insulation material stripped off.

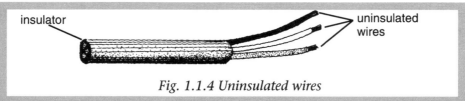

insulator

uninsulated wires

Fig. 1.1.4 Uninsulated wires

Caution

Do not touch uninsulated wires because you may get an electric shock.

Strip about 2 cm of the plastic insulation off each wire inside the cable. The plastic insulation on the wires has different colours.

? Why are the wires insulated?

? What colours are used on the plastic insulation on the three wires?

3   Push the three wires until the main cable is under the cable grip. Connect the 5 cm stripped ends of the wires to the pin heads. Match them correctly using the colours on the plastic insulations covering the wires with the letters on the pin heads. Connect the wire insulated brown to L, the wire insulated blue to N and the wire insulated yellow/green to E. Tighten the screws on each pin head. The wiring in the plug is complete.

Information

The standard plug has three pin heads, two short pin heads and one longer pin head.

The longer pin head at the uppermost is called the **earth pin.** The pin head nearer the fuse is called the **live pin.** The third pin head is the **neutral pin.** The diagram below shows the three pin heads, **live, earth** and **neutral** in their correct positions. The diagram also shows the position of the fuse in the plug.

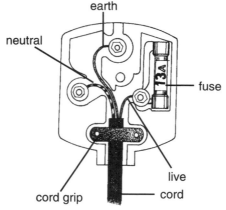

earth

neutral

fuse

live

cord grip

cord

Fig. 1.1.5 Plug

A **fuse** is a thin piece of wire from a mixture of metals which will melt at a high temperature. Below is a diagram of a fuse.

Fig. 1.1.6 Fuse

The fuse is put in the live wire close to the electricity meter, in a box called the **consumer unit**. The position of the fuse is in series in the circuit. The modern way of preventing damage to electrical appliances in homes is by using trip switches. A **trip switch**, like a fuse, is always connected in the live wire and placed in series in the circuit.

A trip switch breaks the circuit automatically when the wires carrying electricity get very hot. It is sometimes called a circuit breaker.

Fig. 1.1.7 A trip-switch

 Written exercise 1.3

From the 'letter table' below search and encircle answers to the following questions. The first is done for you.

M	S	T	R	I	P	S	W	I	T	C	H
A	C	A	B	L	E	A	F	E	H	M	F
T	R	S	U	P	C	M	U	L	R	L	I
W	E	B	W	I	F	L	S	I	E	U	S
E	W	N	E	H	B	I	E	M	E	A	Y
M	D	T	U	S	R	V	U	P	N	U	P
A	R	S	E	R	I	E	S	I	R	A	E
R	I	U	A	L	U	E	T	E	Q	M	D
X	V	B	I	N	E	F	A	E	K	I	P
Y	E	T	E	A	R	T	H	C	N	X	U
B	R	O	W	N	L	I	Q	A	U	D	C

1 How many pin heads has a standard plug?
2 What is the name of the longer pin head in a plug?
3 What prevents electric fires from breaking out in a home?
4 Name the wire on which the trip switch is placed.
5 What is the colour of the plastic insulation for the wire connected to the neutral pin?
6 What is the position of a fuse in a circuit?
7 What is the colour of the plastic insulation for the wire connected to the live pin head?
8 It contains three electric wires.
9 It is used to remove the cover from the plug.
10 Works on the same principle as a fuse.

Activity Set 4

Short circuits

Objectives

By the end of this section you should be able to:
*   explain why electrical wires are insulated.
*   identify a short circuit and state its dangers.

Activities

1   Make a simple circuit with the dry cell and bare copper wires. Using a bare copper wire connect one end of the dry cell to the switch. Get another piece of copper wire, connect it to the other end of the torch bulb and the other end to the switch.

   One end of a bare copper wire is connected to a dry cell and a switch, another bare copper wire is connected to the other end of the torch bulb and the switch.

   Close the switch and hold the bare copper wire.

   ? Do you feel anything? Why?

Caution

Do not touch any bare wire connected to the mains. You can get an electric shock, at times to the extent of getting killed.

2   Make a simple circuit with the dry cell, the torch bulb, the switch and the pieces of bare copper wire. Connect the bulb to one end of the dry cell. Get another bare copper wire and connect the bulb to the switch. Get the third bare copper wire and connect the other end of the dry cell to the switch.

A bulb is connected to one end of the dry cell. Another bare wire connects the bulb to the switch. A third upper wire connects one end of the dry cell to the switch. Close the switch and observe.

[?]   What happens to the bulb? Why?

3   Repeat the set up of the experiment in activity 2. Connect a bare copper wire across the circuit.

[?]   What happens? Why?

4   Repeat the set up for the experiments in activities 2 and 3, but using a different bulb. Close the switch. Connect the bare copper wire across the circuit again and observe.

[?]   What happens to the bulb when the bare copper wire is connected across the circuit?

Information

When electricity flows through a wire, heat is produced. In the bulb, heat is changed to light. When a bare copper wire gets into contact with another bare wire in the circuit, the light in the bulb goes out. The electricity flows through the protruding bare copper wire which has joined the circuit and not through the bulb, making the circuit '**short**'. When this happens we say there is a **short circuit.**

A short circuit occurs when the plastic covering that insulates electrical wires wears out and the wires touch each other. The electricity flows directly from one wire to the other. Short circuits should be prevented.

Overheating of the wires as a result of a short circuit can start a fire in a building. The overheating of wires can also damage electrical appliances, for example, fridges, cookers and television sets.

A person coming into contact with bare wires in a short circuit can get a shock, at times to the extent of getting killed. Death due to electricity is called **electrocution.**

To avoid dangers resulting from short circuits, all electrical wires should be insulated. All insulating materials showing signs of wearing out should be replaced. In some cases, it is advisable that a worn out cable is replaced.

Written exercise 1.4

Complete the sentences below by filling in the blank spaces using the words from the list below.

fridges, insulating, cables, electrocution, heat, televisions, fire, light, short circuit.

1 _____ is produced when electricity flows through a wire.
2 In the bulb heat is changed to _____ .
3 When the plastic covering that insulates electrical wires wears out and wires touch each other, there is a _____ .
4 Overheating of wires as a result of short circuits can start a _____ in a building.
5 Electrical appliances, for example, _____ , cookers and _____ can be damaged as a result of short circuits.
6 Death resulting from electricity is called _____ .
7 Short circuits can be prevented by _____ all electrical wires and replacing worn out _____ .

Activity Set 5

Earthing and lightning

Objectives

By the end of this section you should be able to:
•   describe some causes of lightning and some effects of lightning on plants, animals and buildings.
•   explain why and how some electrical appliances should be earthed.

Activities

1   Look at the illustration of lightning and discuss it in groups.

Fig. 1.1.8 Lightning

1 At what time of the year do you expect to see lightning?
   What will happen to a human being struck by lightning?
   What will happen to a building when struck by lightning?
   What will happen to a tree when struck by lightning?
2 Look at the illustrations of the socket and the plug below.

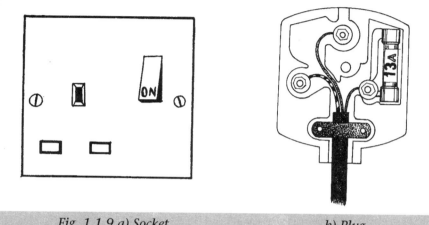

Fig. 1.1.9 a) Socket   *b) Plug*

How many pins are there on the plug?
How many holes are there on the socket?
What is the name of the top and longer pin on the plug?
What is the name of the wire connected to the top longer pin on the plug?
3 In groups, discuss methods of conserving electricity.

Information

Lightning experienced during the rainy season occurs when **positive** and **negative charges** move towards each other through the air. The two charges pull each other, that is, they attract each other. They make electricity that causes a spark which is seen as a flash of lightning.

Lightning can cause damage to property, animals and plants. Lightning can cause damage to a building by starting a fire. When lightning strikes animals, and human beings, they receive a shock and might die.

Plants are also destroyed when lightning strikes them. When lightning strikes a tree, for example, the leaves are burnt, the branches and trunk are split into pieces.

To protect buildings from being struck by lightning, a **lightning conductor**, usually a copper wire, is fixed at the highest point of the building. The lower end of the wire is buried in the earth. When lightning strikes a building, it is conducted through the wire to the earth. The earth wires from electrical appliances are connected to the earth wire in the electrical installation of the house. When there is an electric fault in the electrical appliance, electricity flows through the wire to earth. The earthing connections from all the electrical appliances are taken from the top socket of each plug and led to the earth.

Electricity is costly. It should, therefore, be conserved. We can conserve electricity by switching off all the electrical appliances which are not in use. For example, cookers, heaters, radios, televisions and fans should be switched off and plugs taken out of the sockets when not in use.

Electricity produced by a cell or a group of cells (a battery), can be conserved by switching off the appliance and removing the cells from the circuit. For example, a torch or radio should be switched off and cells removed when not in use.

Solar panels produce electricity. The panels store electricity which is used during the night when there is no sunlight. The diagram below shows solar panels.

Fig. 1.1.10 Solar panel

 Written exercise 1.5

Match items in A with those in B. Follow the example given.

A	B
1 lightning time	electricity
2 cause damage to buildings, animals and plants	switch off and remove cells
3 death by electricity	connected to earth wire

4	earth wires removed from electrical appliances	rainy season
5	earth connections from electrical appliances	irons, fans, heaters and cookers
6	switch off and plug out when not in use	solar panels
7	a group of cells	electrocution
8	radio and the torch not in use	lightning
9	produce electricity from the sunlight	appliance
10	it is costly, therefore, must be conserved	a battery

Chapter

2

PLANTS

Activity Set 1

The flower

Objective

By the end of this section you should be able to:
*   identify and draw the main parts of a flower.

> ### Activities
>
> 1   Go out and select a large flower and bring it to the classroom.
> 2   Examine the flower you have picked. Name the parts you can see.
>   ☑   Does the flower have a scent?
> 3   Pull out the petals and lay them on paper.
>   ▷   What can you see? Write down the parts you can see.
> 4   Using a sharp blade, carefully cut open the ovary.
>   ▷   What can you see?
> 5   Use a lens.
>   ▷   What can you see?

Information

A **flower** is the part of a plant that is responsible for reproduction. It is made up of the **petals, stigma, style, ovary, filament, anther** and **ovules.**

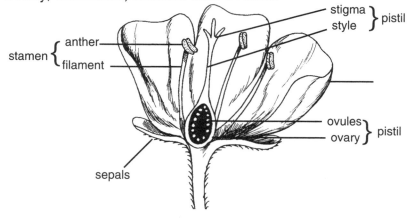

Fig. 2.1.1 Flower

The flower is made up of male and female parts. The male parts are called **stamens.**

The stamen has a long stalk known as a **filament** and an **anther** which has the male cells called **pollen**. The pollen is a powdery substance which is found on the anther at the tip of the filament.

The female part of the flower is called the **pistil**. It consists of a long stalk called the **style**. The style has a sticky tip which is called the **stigma**. At the bottom of the style is the **ovary** which contains **ovules**.

Petals are brightly coloured. At the bottom of the flower, there are small leaves called **sepals.**

 Written exercise 2.1

1   Below is a diagram of a section through a bean flower. Study it carefully and use the list of words below to label the parts which are indicated by arrows.

   petals, ovules, ovary, style, anther, stigma

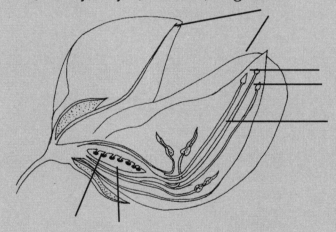

Fig. 2.1.2 A bean flower

2   Write the first part of the sentences from A. Select the second part from B and complete each sentence correctly.

A	B
a) The petals and their sweet scent	the male reproductive part of the flower.
b) The anthers contain pollen which is	by visiting insects or by the wind.

c) Pollen from other flowers is placed on the stigma	the female reproductive parts.
d) The style connects	when it is fertilised by pollen.
e) The ovary contains ovules which are	attract insects.
f) The ovule develops into a seed	the stigma to the ovary.

Activity Set 2

Pollination

Objectives

By the end of this section you should be able to:
* state that pollen is transfered from the anther to the stigma.
* describe how pollination occurs.

Caution
Insects such as bees and wasps sting. Handle them with care.

Activities

1   Walk around your school and observe the different types of flowers.
   ▷   What do you see on the flowers?
   ?   What is it for?
   ?   What is it called?
2   Now observe insects coming to other flowers.
   ?   What kind of insects are they?
   ?   What are the insects doing?
   ?   How many flowers has the insect you have observed visited?
3   Collect as many different flowers as you can and bring them to the classroom. Collect brightly coloured ones. Trap one of the insects observed in activity 2 in a plastic bag. Tie the plastic bag around the stalk of the flower. Look at the insect closely.
   ?   What has it on its body?

Information

In activity 3, you observed an insect and saw a yellow powder on its body. This powder is called pollen. When the insect visits a flower to get **nectar**, the sweet liquid at the base of the flower, the pollen from the anthers sticks to its body. As the insect lands or leaves the flower some of the pollen may stick to the stigma on its body. This transfer of pollen from the anther to the stigma is called **pollination.**

When the insect with the pollen on its body visits another flower it may leave pollen on the stigma of the flower. This type of pollination is called **cross pollination.** This involves transferring pollen grains from flowers of one plant to the flowers of another plant.

Pollen can be carried by insects, wind or water. Flowers that are pollinated by insects are brightly coloured and have a sweet scent. Those that are pollinated by wind are small, not brightly coloured and do not have a scent or nectar, for example, the maize flower.

 Written exercise 2.2

Rewrite this passage in your exercise book using the list below:

big, nectar, inside, pollen, wind, separate, insects, male part, pollination

_____ happens when pollen is carried from the male part to the female part of the flower. Pollen can go from the _____ to the female part of the same flower or from the male part of one flower to other female part of another flower on the same plant. This is self pollination.

When pollen goes from the male part of one flower to the female part of another flower it is called **cross pollination.**

Pollen can be carried by _____ or by wind. _____ pollinated flowers are small, not brightly coloured and do not have a scent or nectar. The flowers usually open before the leaves. A lot of _____ is produced. Insect pollinated flowers are _____ so that they can hold big insects like bees. The male and female parts are usually _____ the flowers, because insects come to collect the pollen. Some insects use a sweet liquid called _____ from inside the flower for food. Some flowers are pollinated by birds or bats.

Activity Set 3

Fertilisation in a flower

Objective

By the end of this section you should be able to:
*   state that the result of fertilisation is a seed.

Activities

1   Take some sugar and mix it with water in a plastic lid or dish to make a strong sugar solution.
2   Choose a fully open flower. Remove one or two stamens from it. You should be able to see plenty of pollen grains on the anthers. Shake some pollen grains onto the surface of the sugar solution in the dish. Stir with a piece of glass or plastic rod.
3   Set the dish in the sun for several hours.
4   Draw what you have seen.
5   Observe a plant that has dry flowers.
     ?   Why has the flower on the plant dried up?
     ▷   What can you see on the plant?
6   Collect as many different types of fruits as you can, such as paw paw, mango, tomato, guava and apple. Cut and open the fruit through the centre.
     ▷   What can you see inside the fruits?
     ?   How are the seeds arranged in the fruits you have collected?
     ?   How many seeds are there in each fruit?

Information

When pollen sticks on the stigma of a flower it starts to grow a long thin tube along the style right down to the ovary. When the tube touches an ovule, the male sex cell called pollen goes down the tube and joins the ovule. The joining of the male sex cell, with the female sex cell, the ovule is called **fertilisation**.

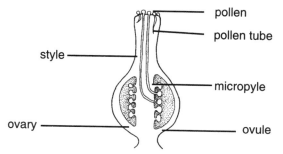

Fig. 2.1.3 Cross section of an ovary

✎ Written exercise 2.3

1   The series of diagrams shows the life cycle of a flowering plant.

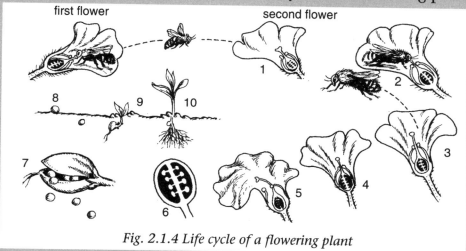

Fig. 2.1.4 Life cycle of a flowering plant

Draw the diagram in your exercise books and write the labels below in their correct places.

ripe fruit   fertilised flower   ovary   seeds   seedling

2   Pollen grains stick to the ————————

3   The pollen ———————— grows down along the style.

4   The pollen grains join with the ———————— in the ovary.

Activity Set 4

How and why should seeds scatter?

Objectives

By the end of this section you should be able to:

- describe different methods of how seeds scatter.
- state the importance of seed dispersal.

Activities

1   In the area around the school or at home, collect fruits and seed boxes.
2   Group them as follows:
Those that are fleshy, for example, apple, paw paw. Those that are dry, for example, bidens pilosa (black jack). Those that have wings, for example, samara. Those that are very light, for example, cotton. In the groups of fruits you have made, name the different ways in which they or their seeds are scattered.
3   Study the picture of the bean plant below:

Fig. 2.1.5 Bean plant

   What has happened to the bean?
   Why?
   What will happen to the seeds?

Information

After fertilisation the seed and fruit are scattered from the plants. This is called **seed dispersal.** Plants like beans experience explosion or self dispersal. In some plants such as mango the whole fruit is dispersed.

In others such as bean, soya beans and sunflower, the seeds are dispersed from the fruit. Fruits and seeds can be dispersed by animals, wind, water and the plant itself. This is called explosion or self dispersal.

In some plants, fruits hold the seeds. Plants, such as tomatoes, are fleshy and attractive. Animals eat the fruit and the seeds pass through their bodies in the faeces or they are spat out from the mouth. Animals help to disperse the seeds in this way. Other examples of seeds dispersed by animals are guavas, oranges, lemons, mangoes and paw paws.

Some fruits have hooks on them. The hooks catch onto the fur of passing animals and later fall off when the animals have gone some distance from the parent plant. An example of a fruit with hooks is the black jack.

Some fruits and seeds are very small and have hairs arranged like a parachute. Others have wings. Such fruits are dispersed by wind. The small hairs and wings help them to be carried over long distances.

In some plants the fruit dries and becomes a hard seed box. The seed box splits open, the hard cover often twists and the seeds are thrown out. There is usually an explosion when this happens. This type of dispersal is called **mechanical dispersal** by explosion.

Some plants grow in or near water, for example, the coconut. Their fruits and seeds are carried by water over long distances.

With the help of dispersal, the new plants are able to grow near the parent plant or further away from the parent plant. New plants are also able to grow in a new place, for example, where the plant has never existed.

✎ Written exercise 2.4

1   Draw the pictures of the different types of fruits and seeds labelled (a-d). Write underneath it the type of dispersal.

a)
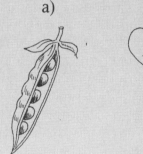
b)
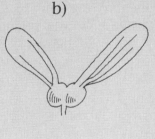
c)

d)
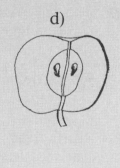

Fig. 2.1.6 Seed dispersal

2   Copy out each of the sentences below and write correctly the mixed up words shown in brackets.
   a)   (lasrepsid) is what happens when fruits and seeds are carried away from the plant that made them.
   b)   Animals eat (sflehy) fruits and the seeds pass through their bodies.
   c)   The wind (sidresspe) seeds which have wings.
   d)   Some plants have pods which (trubs) and scatter their seeds.
   e)   Animals sometimes catch (kedooh) fruit on their fur.

Activity Set 5

Effects of overcrowding in plants and human beings

Objectives

By the end of this section you should be able to:
*   describe effects of overcrowding in plants and human beings.
*   describe seed dispersal and child spacing in human beings.

Activities

1   Think about different fruits you collected in the previous activity when doing the lesson on fertilisation.
       [?]   What would have happened if these fruits were left on the plant?
2   Study the picture below.

Fig. 2.1.7 Banana plants

   [?]   Where did the young plants come from?
   [?]   Do you think that this is the best place for the young plants to grow?
   [?]   Why?
3   Study the picture below.

Fig. 2.1.8 An overcrowded family

? What would happen to the family in the picture?
? Would the members in the family live well?
? Why?

4 Study the picture below.

? Do you think that this is the best place for the young plant to grow?
? Why?

5 Study the picture below:

Fig. 2.1.9 A well spaced family

? Do you think that this is the best way to have a family?
? Why?
? Why do you think that members in this family look happy?

Information

The parent plant **disperses** its fruits and seeds so that they can grow in another place where the conditions may be suitable. To do this, the plant is helped by other factors, such as animals, wind and water.

There are, however, disadvantages when the seeds grow in large numbers near the parent plant. If they all grow near the parent plant, they will be overcrowded and they will not grow well because there will not be enough land, water, shelter and sunlight for them to grow.

This can also be likened to overcrowding in humans. When the family is too large there is need to increase the supply of food. If this is not done the family does not have enough to eat. Shelter also becomes inadequate.

There are advantages of seed dispersal. The seeds are taken further away from the parent plant and overcrowding is avoided. This too can be likened to child spacing in human beings. When children are spaced well, overcrowding is avoided and there is enough shelter and enough food for everyone in the family.

 Written exercise 2.5

1   Look at this picture of a parent plant that has dispersed its seeds.

Describe in your own words, what would happen to the seeds if they all fell near the parent plant.

2   Look at this diagram of an overcrowded family.

Fig. 2.1.10 An overcrowded family

Describe in your own words how the members in the family would live.

Activity Set 6

Vegetative propagation

Objective

By the end of this section you should be able to:
*   describe methods of propagation.

Activities

1   Collect as many of the following plant parts as you can: Irish potato, sweet potato, banana sucker, and onion.
2   Study the plant parts you have collected and describe how they can be grown.
3   Describe how they are planted and what their seeds look like.

Information

Plants do not always reproduce from seeds. Some plants reproduce from tubers, suckers and stems.

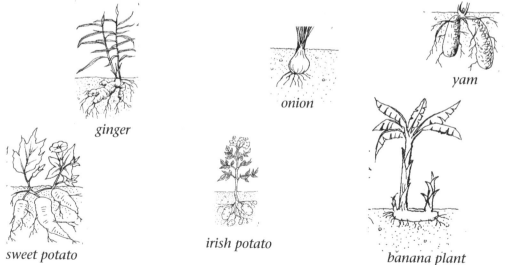

ginger

onion

yam

sweet potato

irish potato

banana plant

Fig. 2.1.11 *Vegetative propagation*

   This type of reproduction in plants is called **vegetative propagation**. It is also called **asexual reproduction**.

The table below shows some types of plants that reproduce asexually.

Name of plant	Picture (illustration)	Method of reproduction
Onion		The bud grows into a new plant using the food stored in leaves.
Sweet potato		Roots grow into tubers.
Strawberry		Runner roots and stem grow under the ground. Stems shoot out later.
Banana		Main plant produces suckers which grow into main plants.
Irish potato		Grows from 'eyes' on the potatoes. These 'eyes' shoot into stems.

 Written exercise 2.6

On page 27, there are illustrations of three plant parts. Opposite each illustration there is a description and the type of plant part, but the descriptions and names are not in the correct order.
    Study the illustrations and the information. Match each illustration to the correct description. Write down the numbers of the drawings and the letters of the descriptions which match them.

Illustration	Description	Type
	A Short, swollen stem with buds, scars and eyes.	Stem tubers
	B Long horizontal stem and scars.	Rhizomes
	C Several swollen roots with some thinner roots and no scars.	Root tubers

Chapter

3

FARMING

Activity Set 1

Financial records of farming activities

Objectives

By the end of this section you should be able to:
* prepare and keep simple financial records of farming activities.
* calculate profit or loss.

Activities

1   Collect invoices for a crop grown or animals kept at your school.
2   List the things on which money was spent to grow this crop or keep the animals. Consider money spent during one month only.
   ❓   How much money was spent?
   ❓   What do you call this money?
3   Collect receipts for the crop or animal you chose in 1 above. Let the receipts be for the month you considered in 2 above.
   ❓   How much money was received?
   ❓   What do you call this money?
   ❓   How much money do you get when you subtract the total money received?
   ❓   What do you call this money?
4   Examine all the invoices of the Production unit for one month. List the things on which money was spent. Set out the information in a table. Add up all the money that was spent during the month you have chosen.
   ❓   What is the total?
   ❓   What do you call this money?
5   Examine all the receipts of the Production unit for the month you chose in 4 above. List all the things on which money was received. Add up all the money that was received.
   ❓   What is the total?
   ❓   What do you call this money?

6   Make a table like the one shown below. Arrange the list for money spent and money taken in. The table below is an example. You can complete the table using the information in activities 4 and 5.

Money spent			Money received		
Date	Item	Amount (K)	Date	Item	Amount (K)

[?]   Why are records kept?

Information

Some farmers specialise in growing one type of crop and record all the expenses met towards producing the crop. After selling the crop they add up all the money spent on, say, two hectares of maize, as shown in the table below:

Money spent			
Date	Item	Quantity	Cost
05/10/95	Bought fertiliser Compound 'D'	8 bags	K80 000.00
05/10/95	Bought Urea	8 bags	K80 000.00
03/01/96	Weeding		K30 000.00
06/10/96	Harvesting		K40 000.00
	– Loading bags		K50 000.00
	– Transport		K50 000.00
25/10/96	– Loading bags		K50 000.00
	– Transport		K50 000.00
	Total costs for 1995/6		K430 000.00

Farmers who do not sell their produce regularly, for example, those who specialise in growing maize, will only have sales to record after each harvest. Such sales as these need to be recorded in a Sales Book for each product, for example, Maize Sales Book or Livestock Sales Book.

The separate books enable the farmer to obtain information about each part of the business quickly and easily. Here is an example of a farmer who grows maize and sells the crop to a Cooperative and Milling Company.

Date	Sold to:	Quantity	Cost
06/10/95	Mweemba Cooperative	60 bags	K1 200 000.00
25/10/95	National Milling Company	50 bags	K1 000 000.00
	Total sales for 1995 season	**110 bags**	**K2 200 000.00**

The farmer is now in a position to determine whether or not he/she made a profit on the farm. For this the farmer opens a special account in the books, called the **profit and loss account**.

Entries in this are made at the end of the farmer's year, that is, when the crop is harvested and sold. For each product the farmer enters the total value of all the sales made during the year and the total amounts paid out in purchases. For our product, maize, the simple profit and loss account would be as follows:

Money spent			Money received		
Date	Item	Amount (K)	Date	Item	Amount (K)
05/10/94	Bought Compound 'D' 8 bags at K10 000 each	K80 000.00	06/10/95	Sold 60 bags of maize at K20 000 each.	K1 200 000.00
5/10/94	Bought urea 8 bags at K10 000 each.	K80 000.00			
6/10/95	Loading bags Transport	K50 000.00 K50 000.00		Sold 50 bags of maize at K20 000 each.	K1 000 000.00

Money spent			Money received		
Date	Item	Amount (K)	Date	Item	Amount (K)
25/10/95	Loading bags	K 50 000			
	Transport	K 50 000			
	Total	K360 000			K2 200 000

The 'Money received by the business' is called the **income** of the farm. The 'Money spent' is called the **expenditure**. The difference between these totals is the profit. The income should be greater than the expenditure for the farm to make a profit for that period of time. If the expenditure is greater than the income, there is a **loss**.

```
Income        K2 200 000.00
Expenditure K   360 000.00
Balance       K1 840 000.00
```

In this example, the income is greater than the expenditure, and so this farm had a profit for that particular year or period.

Farm records are important. They:
- enable the farmer to find out whether he/she is making a profit or loss.
- guide the farmer in planning and making good decisions.
- help a farmer to get loans.
- help farmers in cooperative societies in sharing their bonuses.
- are used in assessing the income tax of the farmer.

 Written exercise 3.1

1 Calculate the profit or loss from the following activities carried out by L. Malita, a farmer.
   02/10/97 Bought vegetable seeds for K1 000.00
   03/10/97 Sale of eggs K3 000.00
   19/10/97 Sale of broilers K200 000.00
   23/10/97 Bought insecticides K10 000.00
   25/10/97 Sale of two pigs K100 000.00
   30/10/97 Bought fertiliser K80 000.00
2 Write *true* or *false* for each of the following:
   a) By using records a farmer can tell whether or not he/she is making a profit.

b)   Records cannot help a farmer to make good decisions.
c)   You can assess the amount of tax a farmer is supposed to pay
        from records.

Activity Set 2

Crop production

Objective

By the end of this section you should be able to:
*   choose a crop to grow in a given area.

Activities

1   Study the bar graphs on rainfall in the two towns in Zambia.

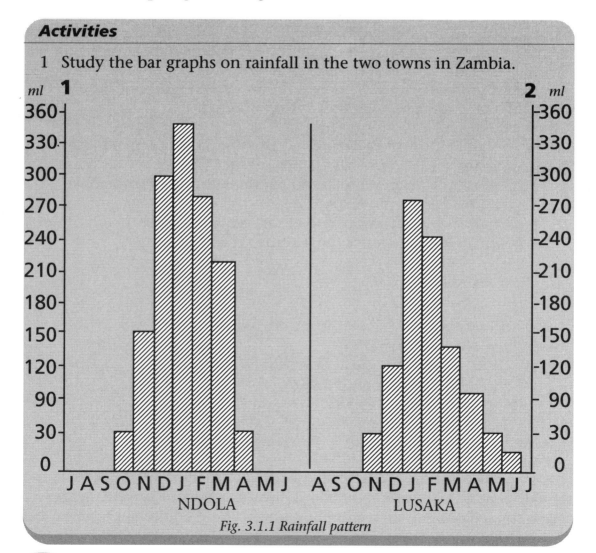

Fig. 3.1.1 Rainfall pattern

> ❓ In which two months did the two towns have very high rainfall?
> ❓ Did the two towns have rain throughout the year? Why?
> ❓ Can you grow maize throughout the year in the two towns? Why?
> ❓ During which months are diseases for plants many in the two towns? Why?

Information

Zambia has wet and dry seasons. Rains begin to fall around the end of October and stop around the end of March or early April. Total rainfall decreases from north to south. Crops to be grown in an area are chosen according to the rainfall (water) requirements. Crops that need a lot of water are grown in areas that receive a lot of rainfall.

Crops that do not need a lot of rainfall (water) are grown in areas that receive little rain.

Zambia is divided into three zones, according to the amounts of rainfall each zone receives. The three zones are shown below.

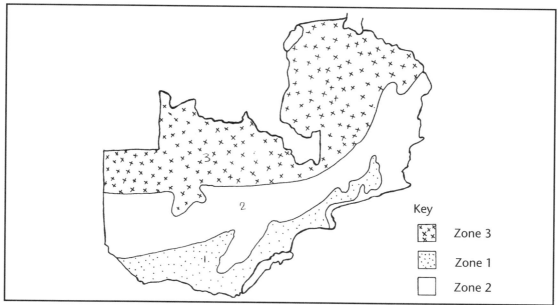

Fig. 3.1.2 Zones of rainfall

Many crops are grown in Zambia. Various factors are considered before a crop is chosen for an area. Some of the factors that are considered are rainfall, type of soil, temperature and diseases. The table on the next page shows some crops grown in Zambia, some of their requirements and some diseases that attack them.

Crop	Type of soil	Rain required	Season grown	Disease	When the disease is common
Maize	loam soil	500-1 250 mm	wet season	diprodea cob rot leaf spot damping off	wet season wet season wet season wet season
Groundnuts	sandy loam soil	500-1 000 mm	wet season	crown rot leaft spot damping off	wet season wet season wet season
Sorghum	loam soil	500-1 000 mm	wet season	leaf blight damping off leaf spot late blight mildew damping off	wet season wet season wet season wet season wet season wet season
Peas	loam soil	600-1 000 mm	all year round	leaf spot mildew	wet season wet season

Crops can only grow if conditions are favourable. Some crops do not grow well when it is very cold. Crops like beans, peas and tomatoes do not grow very well when it is cold.

Other crops do not grow well in the rainy season or when there is too much water because of fungal diseases.

Markets also play an important role in the choice of crops to be grown. Crops that are easy to sell are grown by many farmers. Crops that are difficult to sell are grown by very few farmers. This is so because it is difficult for farmers to earn an income quickly from a crop that is difficult to sell. There are very few people who need such crops. These crops fetch low prices and as a result very few farmers grow them.

Written exercise 3.2

1   Study the bar graph below and answer the questions that follow.

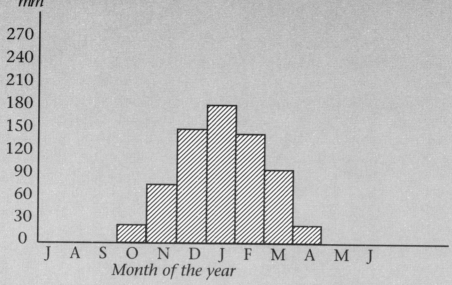

Fig. 3.1.3 Rainfall pattern

a)   Write down the months which had no rain.
b)   How much rain fell in December?
c)   In which months would fungal diseases be most common?
d)   How can you reduce fungal diseases?

2   Which crop can you recommend for growing in Zone 1 on the map of Zambia shown on page 33?

Activity Set 3

Livestock production

Objective

By the end of this section you will be able to:
•   choose livestock to keep in a given area.

Activities

1   Study the map of Zambia on page 36 and answer the questions that follow.

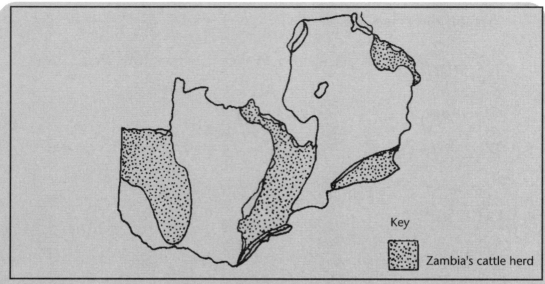

Fig. 3.1.4 Cattle location

[?] Which animals are found in the shaded areas on the map of Zambia?
[?] Why are these animals concentrated in these areas?
[?] Why is livestock kept?

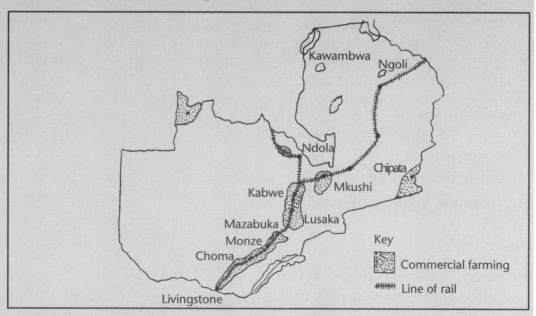

Fig. 3.1.5 Commercial farming areas

2   Study the map of Zambia shown above and answer the following question.

[?]   What takes place in the shaded areas on the map of Zambia? Why?

Information

Diseases transmitted by ticks make it difficult to rear livestock like cattle. In the Southern province there was an outbreak of a tick borne disease some time back and many cattle died. This made it difficult for farmers to rear cattle in the province until the disease was brought under control. So, the distribution of livestock in the country depends on several factors. The most important of these factors are discussed below.

Market
Commercial farmers specialising in livestock must have markets for their produce. So these farms must be near towns, where the eggs and meat can be sold quickly.

Disease
Cattle cannot be reared in areas where there are tsetse flies. Only special breeds of cattle are resistant to the disease carried by the tsetse fly. The indigenous (local) breeds of cattle are slightly resistant to the disease transmitted by tsetse flies.

The tsetse fly carries the **trypanosome**, a tiny animal (germ) which lives in the bloodstream of cattle. It causes the disease called **trypanosomiasis**, which is a very serious widespread cattle disease.

Transport
Large farms are usually near good roads, so that trucks can take the produce to markets or to the factory for processing.

 Written exercise 3.3

1   Draw an outline map of Zambia and mark on the map the areas of the country where it is not possible to keep cattle.
2   Mention three breeds of cattle found in Zambia. For each breed, list two provinces in which the breed would be found. Copy the table into your exercise book and then fill in the answer:

Breed	Province
Barotse	1 ————
	2 ————

Tonga	1 _____
	2 _____
Angoni	1 _____
	2 _____

3 Write this passage about farming in your exercise book. Choose the correct words from the list provided to complete the blanks in the passage.

market, roads

Commercial farms specialising in livestock must be near _____ . So these farms must be close to the _____ where products can be sold quickly.

Activity Set 4

Harvesting

Objective

By the end of this section you should be able to:
* describe how to harvest various crops and their storage at the farm and national level.

Activities

1 Discuss when to harvest cabbage, tomato, beans, rape, groundnuts, and maize.
  - ？ Why should crops be harvested?
  - ？ How are the crops carried home from the field or taken to the market?
2 Study the chart on crop storage facilities and harvesting methods.
  - ？ Which crops can be stored in each facility?
  - ？ Why are crops stored?
  - ？ How are the crops you have discussed stored at the farm and at national level?
  - ？ How are the crops you have discussed harvested?

Information

Study the table showing some of the crops grown in Zambia. The table shows when harvesting of the crops is supposed to start. The table also gives brief information on how each crop can be harvested.

Crop	Harvesting period	Method
Cabbage	8-16 weeks from seed sowing	Cut when the heads are fine, young and tender, before they crack. Cut above soil level.
Rape	8 weeks from seed sowing	Pick leaves regularly. Picking can go on for another 8 weeks.
Spinach	8 weeks from seed sowing	Cut off the plants completely.
Runner beans	12 weeks from sowing	Pick pods regularly.
Peas	8-12 weeks from sowing or less depending on the variety and weather	Pick pods as often as possible.
Carrots	8-9 weeks from seed sowing	Remove the best developed roots and leave room for the remainder to develop.
Beetroot	8 weeks from seed sowing	Lift the roots during a dry spell. Do not damage the roots. Twist off the leaves.
Radish	12-14 days from seed sowing	Lift the larger roots first.
Tomato	10-12 weeks from sowing	Remove fruits by breaking the joint in the stalk using the thumb. Pick regularly.
Onion	36-40 weeks from sowing	Pull and leave them to dry off before collecting for storing in shady airy spots. Pull them in September to November.

Leek	20 weeks from seed sowing	Pull them from the ground or use a garden fork.
Groundnuts	22 weeks from seed sowing	Dig out the pods and let them dry.
Maize	26 weeks from seed sowing	Pick the cobs when the husks are brown and dry. A machine can be used to harvest the crop.

Crops are ready for harvesting at different times. Each crop may be harvested in a different way. Crops need to be harvested correctly or they get damaged. Damaged crops have a low value. If some crops are not harvested at the right time their value is lowered. The yield of a crop harvested late may also be lowered, for example, soya beans. Loss of yield in soya beans is high if it is harvested late due to shaltering.

After crops are harvested they are transported in various ways. Small scale farmers may use human labour. They may carry the produce on their heads in baskets.

Medium scale farmers may use animals like oxen to pull carts loaded with produce.

Commercial farmers may use lorries and tractors pulling trailers loaded with produce.

Depending on the size of the produce harvested it may be stored in pots, calabashes and granaries in the village. At national level agricultural produce may be stored in silos.

Chemicals may be added to the stored produce. This is done to protect it from pests. This makes it possible for the produce to stay for a long time before it goes bad. After harvesting food crops are stored to reduce food shortages.

✎ **Written exercise 3.4**

1   Match each crop in column X with its correct harvesting time.

X	Y
rape	26 weeks
groundnuts	22 weeks
tomato	8 weeks

	X	Y
	onion	10 weeks
	maize	36 weeks

2 Write *true* or *false* for each of the following statements.
   a) Different crops sown at the same time can be harvested at the same time.
   b) If a crop is not harvested at the right time its value falls.
   c) A cart can be used to transport harvested crops.
   d) Adding chemicals to stored crops makes them stay long before going bad.

Activity Set 5

Population size and food supply

Objective

By the end of this section you should be able to:
*   relate food supply to size of population.

Information

In a town or country when the number of people increases, the amount of food required also increases. If the increase is rapid food may not be enough for all the people in the town or country. Some people will go without food. There may be famine. Food produced by farmers or bought from outside the country will not be enough.

   If the number of people in a town is small the farmers will find it easy to produce food for a small number of people. This means that there would be no need to buy some extra food from another town or country to feed them. This reduces money spent to buy food from outside.

 Written exercise 3.5

1 Write *true* or *false* for each of the following statements.
   a) When people are few in a family the amount of food required increases.
   b) When the number of people increases rapidly in a country some people can go hungry.

2   Study the graph below and answer the questions that follow.

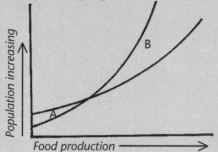

Fig 3.1.6 Effect of population increase on food production

a) What can you say about the amount of food supplied at A and B in the graph?

Activity Set 6

Irrigation

Objectives

By the end of this section you should be able to:
*   explain why crops are irrigated.
*   describe irrigation of crops.
*   state the effects of irrigation.

Activities

1   Study the picture below.

Fig. 3.1.7 Type of farming method

? What is happening in the picture?

? Why?

? What name can you give to the system used in the picture?
Name other systems used to provide water to crops.

? Why should you not overwater crops?

? What happens when you overwater soil?

Information

In a country like Zambia, where there is a long dry season, people grow crops only in the rainy season. Even in the rainy season, some parts of Zambia do not get enough rainfall for crops to live and grow. To grow crops all the year round, there must be a way of storing water and then bringing it to the fields when it is needed. Water can be brought from places like rivers, lakes and boreholes where it is plenty, to the parts that need it. This is called **irrigation**.

Irrigation makes it possible for farmers to grow crops throughout the year. This means that crop production can be increased on the farm.

There are several effects of irrigation on the soil. Salts may increase. Crops and plants do not grow well on the soils that have a lot of salts. **Nutrients** may be washed down the **subsoil** where some crops and other plants can not reach them. This can result in poor growth of some crops and plants.

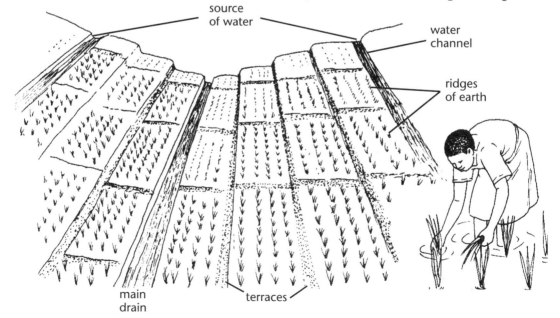

Fig. 3.1.8 Flood irrigation

As nutrients collect in the subsoil, it develops a hard layer which does not allow water to pass easily. This results in waterlogging. Since most crops and plants do not favour waterlogged soils, they die.

Bacteria and fungi do not favour soils that have a lot of salts. So, bacteria and fungi may be killed by the salts. This makes the soil poor in **humus** since the bacteria and fungi make **humus**.

✎ Written exercise 3.6

1   Choose words from the list provided to complete the passage below. Write it in your exercise book.

salts, use, surface, drains, plants, dry, irrigation, accumulating, sub

All _____ need water to grow. Zambia has a long _____ season. If plants are to be grown all year round, _____ is necessary. Irrigation water washes _____ to the _____ soil and results in salts _____ there.

2   This picture shows part of Nakambala sugar estate in the Southern province. Study it and say which method of irrigation is being used.

Fig. 3.1.9 Part of Nakambala sugar estate

Activity Set 7

Loss of soil fertility

Objectives

By the end of this section you should be able to:

- discuss the effects of overusing chemical fertilisers in the field.
- describe effects of soil erosion.
- suggest methods of preventing soil erosion.

Activities

1   Study the picture of a field below.

Fig. 3.1.10 Maize field

[?]   Is the maize in this field growing well? Why?

2   Look around the school grounds and check on the damage caused by rain.

[?]   What damage has been caused?

3   Study the charts before you.

[?]   What is happening to the soil on the bare land?

[?]   Can crops grow well on this land? Why?

[?]   Can you think of some ways of stopping this damage?

4   Make a model hill by piling some sand or soil into a heap. Pat the sides with your hands to make them smooth.

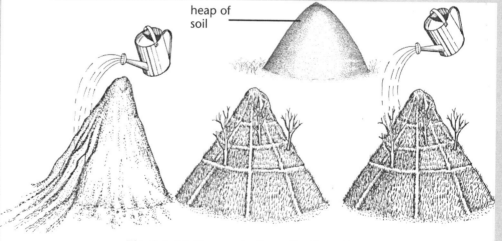

heap of soil

Fig. 3.1.11 Demonstration of soil erosion

Use a spade to cut some square pieces of grass turf. Cover the face of the hill with them. Fit them closely together and press them down to make a grass covered slope. Stick a few twigs into the hill to represent trees.

Use the watering can to make rain fall onto the hill. Observe how the vegetation you have put protects the surface of the hill.

?   Is a lot of soil washed down?

?   Why?

Information

The application of too much fertilisers such as ammonium nitrate, ammonium sulphate and urea make the soil bad for growing crops. When these fertilisers are used, too many clay particles that hold plant nutrients are destroyed. This makes the soil lose plant nutrients. Roots of crops may be poisoned and die. The bacteria and fungi which make dead animals and plants change to humus are killed. All these make the crops grow poorly like those in the field shown in the just ended activity.

When the soil is left bare and it rains, rain drops hit it, causing pieces of soil to splash up. These pieces are washed away and lost when water flows. Small channels form as water runs over the surface. After some time, gullies are formed.

When the soil is bare wind may blow on it. The wind blows away the soil particles from bare land. The carrying away of soil by running water or wind is called **soil erosion.** Some causes of soil erosion are discussed below:

Burning the bush
When people burn trees and bushes to clear land, the soil is left exposed to rain water and wind. Running water can carry soil away. Wind can blow soil away.

Overgrazing
If too many cattle or goats use an area of land, they eat all the grass and loosen the soil. The soil is then exposed to the wind which can blow it away.

Clearing crops
If all crop plants are removed when harvesting, the soil may be left open to the wind and rain.

Cultivating on a slope
On sloping land, heavy rains cause powerful **run off** (flowing water). If the soil on such a slope is cultivated, the running water finds it loosened and carries it down the slope.

Making sure that the washing away of soil by water or the blowing away of soil by wind is reduced is called **soil conservation**.

There are many ways of controlling soil erosion. Some of the ways are listed below:

*   Keep a cover of vegetation on the land.
*   Protect the soil from the action of wind and water. If an area of land is open to wind, plant trees in rows. Trees reduce the force of the wind.
*   Plough the land along the line of contours when cultivating slopes. If a slope is used for crops, plant different crops in strips along the slope. Some plants have loose root systems, while others have roots which bind tightly with the soil. The tightly binding plants hold the soil when water tries to wash it away.
*   Prepare terraces on land which is sloping. The terraces should be flat so as to reduce water run off.
*   Make ridges across a slope. The heaped up soil prevents loss of water and topsoil.

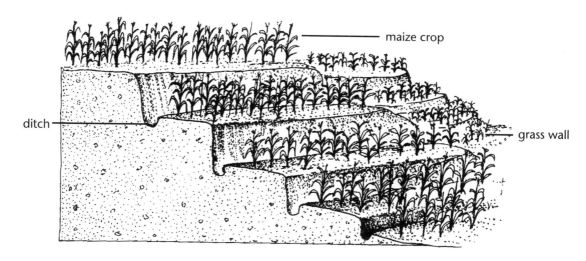

Fig. 3.1.12 Terracing

 Written exercise 3.7

1   In your exercise book make two columns and give them the following titles: **causing soil erosion** and **controlling soil erosion**.
    Under the title **causing soil erosion** write three causes of soil erosion.
    Under the title **controlling soil erosion** write **three** ways in which you can control each cause you have listed under the title **causing soil erosion**.

2   Complete the statements below using words from the following list.
    die, leaching, humus, aeration, destroyed, infertile
    When you overuse fertilisers, bacteria and fungi in the soil
    _____ . These help to decompose dead plants and animals
    into _____ . When you overuse fertilisers clay particles
    are _____ making the soil _____ .

Activity Set 8

The Cooperative

Objectives

By the end of this section you should be able to:
*   discuss membership for a cooperative society.
*   explain how a cooperative society works.
*   state benefits of joining a cooperative society.

Activities

An officer from the Ministry of Agriculture or from one of the cooperatives
will talk to you about cooperative societies.
1   After the officer has talked to you, make sure that you can answer
    the following questions:
    ▢   What is a cooperative society?
    ▢   How can one become a member of a cooperative society?
    ▢   How does a cooperative society work?
    ▢   What are the benefits of joining a cooperative society?
2   If you cannot answer the questions in activity 1 ask the officer the
    same questions. Write down the answers to the questions.

Information

A cooperative society is a registered organisation of people who work
together for common economic benefits. Membership to a cooperative
society is open. It is free for anyone to join. Members are not forced to join
a cooperative society. They are free to join or leave it. Some of the functions
of a cooperative society are to:

- arrange for the production and marketing of produce.
- enable members to get financial help in the form of loans.
- give advice on or information to members about improved techniques to expand production.
- provide improved collective storage and processing of members' produce.
- stock and sell produce to members at reduced prices.
- offer saving facilities on money deposited.
- give technical advice on how to keep account books.
- secure agricultural inputs at reasonable prices for their members.
- bargain for better prices for their members.

There are many benefits members of a cooperative society get. Farmers spend less money on inputs because of buying in large quantities. They can obtain credit facilities, to help them in their farming activities much more easily. It is easier for a cooperative society to secure agricultural inputs such as fertilisers, seeds and pay for them at the end of the marketing season than when it is done individually. Members have a big bargaining power for better prices and conditions. Members have easy access to agricultural inputs such as feeds, fertiliser and seeds. Agricultural information or knowledge is easily disseminated among members. Transportation and marketing of produce is made easy. Improved storage and processing is possible.

✎ Written exercise 3.8

Complete the blank spaces in the following statements, using the following words.

open, registered, prices, credit, bargaining, inputs

A cooperative is a _____ organisation. Membership to a cooperative society is _____. Farmers spend less money on _____ because of buying in bulk. Farmers can obtain _____ to help in their farming activities easily. Members have big _____ power for better _____ .

Chapter 4

FORCES

Force of gravity

Objectives

By the end of this section you should be able to:
* carry out simple experiments on gravity.
* discuss gravity.

Activities

1 In groups, go outside and find some space. Hold a pen and let it go.
  ❓ What happens to the pen?
  ❓ Try other things like a book, a stone, a piece of paper and a piece of cloth.
  ❓ What happens to all these things when you let them go?

Fig. 4.1.1 Falling objects

2   In pairs, try to jump up as high as you can.
    ❓   What happens when you jump?
3   This time try to jump up and stay up.
    ❓   Did you make it? Why?
4   Go into the play ground with your friend. One at a time, kick the ball higher up and observe it.
    ❓   What happens to the ball?
5   Let your friend kick the ball now and observe it.
    ❓   What happens to the ball? Why?
6   Go back to your classroom and do the same activities while inside the classroom. Take care not to damage school property.
    ❓   What happens to the objects?
    ❓   Is it the same as outside?
    ❓   What do you think will happen if you did the same activities in Zimbabwe, Malawi or Japan?
    ❓   Why do things fall towards the earth?

Information

Think of the things you do every day. You pull up a chair to sit down. You also push doors and windows to open and close them. You lift things. You kick and throw balls and other things. Whenever you pull, push, lift or turn anything, you are exerting **force**. There are several different kinds of forces in the world. One of these forces is the **pull of gravity**. The earth exerts a force on all objects. This force called **gravity** is a pulling force.

The force of gravity makes all objects thrown up to come down. This force of gravity on an object is also known as the **weight of the object.** The force of gravity is the same everywhere on earth. However, this force of gravity weakens or becomes less as we go further away from the earth into space. It also reduces slightly as you move away from the poles of the earth to the equator. For example, the pull of gravity on the moon is very little. This is why the **astronauts** who land on the moon are sometimes able to float in space.

✎ **Written exercise 4.1**

Match the sentences in A with the correct ending in B.

A	B
1 A force is either	the more stretches the spring balance.
2 Weight is a force	used to measure weight.

3	Weight reduces as	a push or a pull.
4	The force of gravity	upon the force of gravity pulling on it.
5	A spring balance is	you go away from the earth into space.
6	The name Newton	due to the pull of the earth's gravity.
7	The more matter an object has	acts on all objects eveywhere on earth comes from Sir Isaac Newton.

Activity Set 2

Weight

Objective

By the end of this section you should be able to:
* show that the pull of the earth on objects is its weight.

Activities

Follow the instructions below to make a spring balance.
1   Use a flat plank or a metre ruler. If you use a plank, make markings on it of about 1 cm apart. Markings should run from top to bottom. Hang a spring or an elastic band in front of the ruler. Make sure that the spring hangs up to 0 cm on the ruler.
2   Hang the objects you have on the spring, one at a time. Use the following objects: **cup, ruler, duster, pen, shoe**.
?   What happens to the spring each time? Why?
3   Record your findings in the table below:

Name of object	Length

?   Which objects stretched the spring most?
?   Which one stretched the spring the shortest?
?   Why did you have these differences?

Information

Objects are pulled towards the earth by the force of gravity. This force on objects is called the **weight** of an object. The weight of an object is therefore the force that is exerted on it by the earth. We can measure the weight of an object with a balance called a **spring balance**. The weight of an object depends on the amount of mass in it.

The unit of measure of weight is the **newton**. The name newton comes from a famous scientist, Sir Isaac Newton. He conducted many experiments on the nature and behaviour of forces. People often confuse weight with **mass.** They talk about weight when they mean mass. The difference is that **mass** is the amount of matter in an object and is measured in **kilograms** while weight is the force exerted on an object by the earth. This force is sometimes called **gravitational force** and is measured in newtons.

 Written exercise 4.2

Use a spring balance to measure things we use in a classroom and make a block graph. Use the table below:

Object	Reading
duster	
Science book	
pencil	
pen	
one shoe	
empty box of chalk	
teacher's watch	
classroom key	

Activity Set 3

Principle of moments

Objective

By the end of this section you should be able to:
* use a marked stick or beam to show the principles of balancing.

Activities

1   In groups, discuss the following statement. John weighs 80 newtons while Jane weighs 60 newtons.
    ?   How can the two pupils balance on a sea-saw?
2   Set up a beam balance as follows:
    Put a metre ruler over a small round log so that it balances as shown:

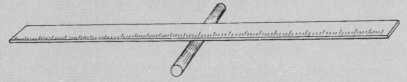

Fig. 4.1.2 Beam balance

In calculating moments the units should or must be correct. The units are **newton** for a force and **metre** for distance. When newtons and metres are multiplied together, the answer is the newton metre.

   Moments are measured with a beam balance. To balance the moments, the beam must be balanced.

3   Take a duster and place it on the ruler 30 cm away from the log on the left.
    ?   What happens to the ruler?
4   Take a similar duster and place it on the ruler 30 cm on the right side of the log.
    ?   What happens to the ruler?
5   Add one or more dusters on the left of the log.
    ?   What happens to the ruler again?
6   Now move the duster on the right side slowly away from the log.
    ?   What is happening to the ruler?
    ?   What happens when you place the duster 60 cm away from the log? Why?

If the beam is balanced, then the forces on one side of the pivot should balance the other side of the pivot. This means that the **moment** of the forces on one side of the beam is equal to the **moment** of the forces on the other side.

   To find the **moment** of a force, we multiply the weight of an object by the distance from the pivot.

   Moment = force (in **newtons**) × distance from pivot (in **metres**).

   Two weights, one big and the other small can balance on a beam balance if they are placed at different distances from the pivot as shown on the next page.

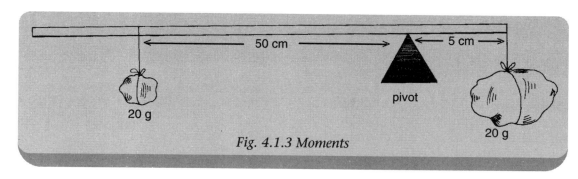

Fig. 4.1.3 Moments

Information

We can calculate the **moments** of two objects as:
Moment = Force (weight) × distance.

Moments on the left	=	Moments of the right
20 N × 2 m		10 N × 4 m
= 40 N m		= 40 N m

The moments on the left are equal to the moments on the right. Since a moment is the **turning effect** of a force, we can also say that the turning effect on the left must be equal to the turning effect on the right in order for the forces to balance.

✎ Written exercise 4.3

1   Copy out and fill in the missing words.
   a)   The turning effect of a force is its _____.
   b)   This depends on the _____ used and the _____ from the pivot.
   c)   To calculate the turning effect of a force, we multiply the _____ by the _____ from the pivot.
2   Calculate the moments in the following example:

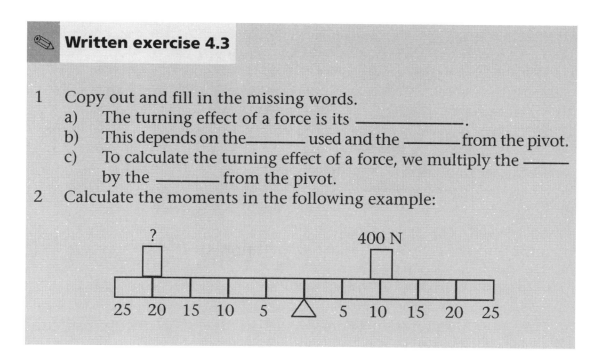

Activity Set 4

Uses of balancing

Objective

By the end of this section you should be able to:
*   describe how balancing is used in everyday life.

Activities

Study the pictures below:

Fig. 4.1.4 Balancing

1 Identify the things in the picture.
   ☐   Where are they used?
   ☐   Do the things in the picture use balancing in order to work?
2 Explain how the things in the picture are made to balance.

Information

The principle of moments or balancing forces is very important in our everyday life. We use this principle in many ways. For example, marketeers and shop owners use beam balances in finding the masses of goods. Other simple machines like levers and pulleys also use this principle of moments. In industries, balancing is also used in many ways. One example is in the **car hoist**. The hoist may lift the car when it is being serviced.

The principle of balancing is also used by aircraft. When an aircraft is moving in the air at high speed, the weight of the aircraft is balanced by the lift from the wings and air resistance is balanced by the power from the engine.

Apart from the examples given, there are several other uses of balancing.

✎ **Written exercise 4.4**

Fill in the blank spaces using the words below:
   lift, levers, car hoist, wings, sea-saw, shopkeepers, pulleys, marketeers, masses

1   Balancing is used by ——————— and ———————to compare the ——————— of commodities.
2   In industries, a ——————— is an example of balancing.
3   Simple machines such as ——————— and ——————— also use balancing.
4   An aircraft's weight is balanced by the ——————— from the ——————— .
5   Another example of balancing is the ——————— used in the play park.

Chapter 5

MATTER

Activity Set 1

Mining in Zambia

Objective

By the end of this section you should be able to:
* describe how minerals are mined in Zambia.

Activities

1 Study the pictures below and describe what is happening in each picture.

Fig. 5.1.1 Quarrying

Fig. 5.1.2 Open pit mining

Fig. 5.1.3 Deep mining

2 Discuss the differences in the pictures and the activities that are taking place in the pictures.
3 Name places in Zambia where such activities take place.
4 Now look at the map of Zambia on page 60 and answer the questions that follow.

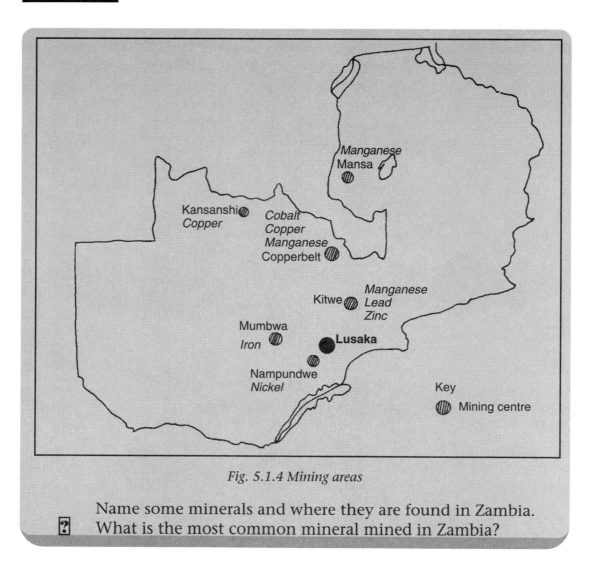

Fig. 5.1.4 Mining areas

Name some minerals and where they are found in Zambia.
What is the most common mineral mined in Zambia?

Information

Mining is Zambia's chief source of income. Minerals are mined almost throughout the country. **Copper** is the main mineral mined. It is mined on the **Copperbelt**. There are three methods of extracting minerals in Zambia.

Shaft mining or deep mining

This type of mining is done in the Copperbelt towns of Kitwe, Luanshya and Mufulira. Shafts are sunk deep in the ground. Tunnels are cut to the levels where the rock containing the mineral can be found. The rock containing the mineral is called **metal ore**.

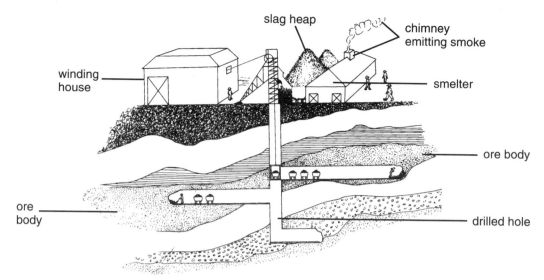

Fig. 5.1.5 Shaft mining

Explosives are then placed in holes drilled in the rock containing the metal ore and blasted. After the rock has been blasted, it is taken for smelting.

Open cast mining

This is done in an open mine. The metal ore is blasted on the earth's surface by use of explosives. The blasted rock is then loaded onto huge trucks and taken for smelting.

Fig. 5.1.6 Open cast mining

This type of mining is mostly done in Chingola at the Chingola Open pit mine.

The quarry method

Minerals such as coal are mined by using the quarry method.

Written exercise 5.1

1   Draw a map of Zambia and show where the following minerals are mined: **copper, zinc, lead, coal** and **emeralds**.
2   The three types of mining in Zambia are ————— , —————— and ————— .

Activity Set 2

How copper is mined

Objective

By the end of this section you should be able to:
•   describe how copper is mined in Zambia.

Activities

1   Discuss in groups and list down the names of minerals mined in Zambia.
    ❓   Which is the most common mineral?
    ❓   What is Zambia's chief source of income?
2   In groups discuss how the mineral is mined.
3   Look at the picture below and discuss what is happening.

Fig. 5.1.7 Mining

Information

In the previous lesson you learned how minerals are mined in Zambia. Copper is mostly mined on the Copperbelt, and this is done in stages. After the rock ore has been mined, the pieces are put in a machine called the **ball mill.** This has big steel balls which roll and break the ore into very small pieces. These very small pieces which are now in the form of powder are mixed with water.

The next stage is the removal of all copper from the ore to leave other minerals. The mixture of the powder mineral and water is put in a tank full of oily water. Air is blown into the tank to make bubbles and the mixture is stirred continuously. When this is done, the copper mineral sticks to the bubbles and floats onto the surface. The other materials sink to the bottom. This process is called **floatation.**

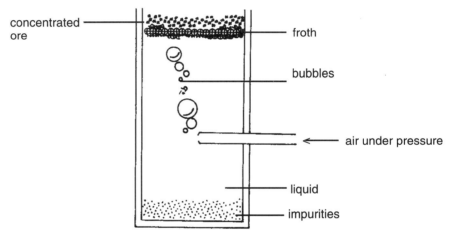

concentrated ore — froth — bubbles — air under pressure — liquid — impurities

Fig. 5.1.8 Floatation tank

The floating copper is removed from the tank and at this stage it is called **concentrate.** The concentrate is later mixed with acid and electricity is made to pass through the mixture to make copper metal plates. This stage is called **electrolysis.**

The copper is now ready for use. It is transported to where it can be used for different purposes.

 Written exercise 5.2

1   The passage below describes what happens in a floatation tank for concentrated copper ore. Some words have been left out. Fill in the words using those provided in the list.

surface, stick, bubbles, floatation, blown, tank, copper mineral, copper ore, electrolysis

A stream of air is ———— into a —————— of oily water which is stirred. The air causes ———— to rise to the surface with bubbles of air on the —————— of the water. This method is known as ————.

2 The last stage of refining copper is known as ——————.
3 The rock containing the copper is called ——————.

Activity Set 3

Uses of copper

Objective

By the end of this section you should be able to:
• list the properties and uses of copper.

Activities

1 Discuss in groups and list some of the things made out of copper.
   • Name those found in the classroom.
   • Name those found in your home.
   • Name those found elsewhere.
2 Discuss what copper is used for.

Information

Copper is a natural metal and has many properties. The pictures on page 65 show some of its properties.

Copper is a **good conductor** of electricity, therefore it can be used in electric appliances.

Copper is non-magnetic and has a high melting point.

There are many uses of copper. It does not wear away and it is used widely in the manufacture of many modern pieces of equipment and machines,

Fig. 5.1.9 a) Copper wires   *b) Copper sheets*

for example, motor car parts, aircraft parts, ships, computers, boilers, radiators, refrigerators and electromagnets.

Many craftsmen use it to make jewellery such as rings, bracelets, necklaces and earrings. It is also used in making decorative ornaments for the home and other places like offices and hotels.

✎ Written exercise 5.3

1   Some of the properties of copper are ——————, —————— and ——————— .

2   Some of the uses of copper are ——————, ———————, ——————— and ——————— .

Activity Set 3

Effects of mining on the environment

Objective

When you come to the end of this section you should be able to:
*   describe the effects of mining on the environment.

Activities

1   Study the following pictures very carefully.

A

Fig. 5.1.10 Pollution

B

Fig. 5.1.11 Open pit mine

C

Fig. 5.1.12 Barren land

D

Fig. 5.1.13 Mine dump

- ❓ What is happening in each of the pictures **A** to **D**?
- ❓ What might happen to all the life in the river shown in picture **A**?
- ❓ What might happen to the air surrounding the area shown in picture **B**?
- ❓ What could have led to the land in picture **C** being barren?

Information

Mining activities bring about **pollution** to the environment. When minerals are being refined fumes of gases are released in the air. These fumes go out through chimneys into the air.

These fumes are poisonous. When they are released into the air, they mix with the water vapour which turns into rain. In this way rainwater becomes polluted. When the water vapour condenses and falls as rain, it falls with the dissolved poisonous fumes. This rain mixed with fumes is called **acid rain**.

This rain will in turn pollute the land, plants and water. The land becomes barren and nothing grows on it. Plant life becomes destroyed and life in the water is also destroyed.

Some mineral wastes are pumped into nearby rivers. The water in these rivers is then polluted. The fish and plants living in these rivers die and the water cannot be used by humans and other animals. Other mineral wastes are poured on the land to make heaps or slags of waste.

This slag takes up a lot of land which could be used for farming and building. When rain falls, the water carries with it part of the waste from the slag into the surrounding land, thus polluting it.

Pollution of the environment can have an adverse effect on human, animal and plant life if it is not controlled.

 Written exercise 5.4

Answer the following questions in your exercise book.
1   Write down in your own words, what the word **pollution** means.
2   What happens if the air is polluted?
3   Which diseases are you likely to suffer from if you stay near a mine?
4   Draw pictures to show pollution and its effects in the air, on the land and in water.

Activity set 1

Chapter 6

DISEASES

Common diseases in Zambia

Objectives

By the end of this section you should be able to:
* identify common diseases in Zambia.
* make a report on how they are caused and spread and how they can be treated and prevented.

Activities

1. In groups, discuss common diseases in your area.
   - ? What are their names?
   - ? What causes the diseases identified?
2. Your teacher would have asked you to bring a chart showing local diseases from a clinic near your school. Study the chart and answer the following questions.
   - ? How many diseases are there?
   - ? What are their names?
   - ? Which ones affect most people?
   - ? Which ones can be spread from one person to another and how?
   - ? How can they be prevented?
   - ? How can they be treated?
3. In groups of three or four, draw a table and record the common diseases using the following table as your guideline.

Name of disease	Cause	Does it spread easily?		Prevention	Treatment
		Yes	No		

Information

A disease is an **illness**. An illness usually has **signs** and **symptoms** which show that a person is not feeling well. Some of these signs are tiredness, weakness, aches, pains, swellings, vomiting, running stomach (diarrhoea) or a high body temperature. Sometimes diseases may cause death.

Fig. 6.1.1 Sick persons

Some diseases affect people more often than others. Some examples of common diseases are cholera, dysentry, malaria, tuberculosis, coughs and colds.

Diseases are caused by many different things. Some are caused by tiny organisms called **bacteria** or **viruses** or **germs** while others are caused by bad feeding habits or **malnutrition.**

Examples of diseases which are caused by bacteria are tuberculosis, pneumonia and malaria. Diseases which are a result of malnutrition are kwashiorkor and marasmus.

Diseases can be categorised into two main types: **non-infectious** and **infectious** diseases. Non-infectious diseases do not spread from a sick person to a healthy person. Infectious diseases are spread from a sick person to a healthy person. An example of a non-infectious disease is a mental illness called **epilepsy**. Infectious diseases include cholera, dysentry, typhoid, tuberculosis and meningitis.

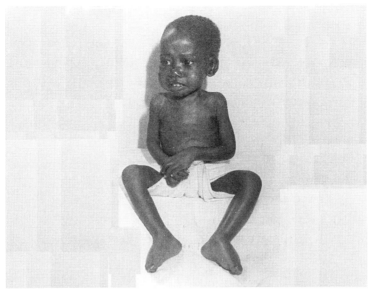

Fig. 6.1.2 Child suffering from kwashiorkor

Study the table below. It shows names of some of the common infectious and non-infectious diseases and what causes them. Copy this table in your exercise book and fill in the prevention and treatment columns as has been done for diarrhoea.

Disease	Infectious/ non-infectious	Cause	Prevention	Treatment
Diarrhoea	infectious	germs	Improve on personal hygiene.	Give plenty of oral rehydration solution.
Malaria	non-infectious	germs		
Tuberculosis	infectious	germs		
Cholera	infectious	germs		
Kwashiorkor	non-infectious	lack of protein in one's diet		
Asthma	non-infectious	an allergy or hereditary		
Meningitis	infectious	germs		

Written exercise 6.1

Write *true* or *false* for each of the following statements.
1   Oral rehydration solution restores water and salts in a person suffering from diarrhoea.
2   Kwashiorkor is an infectious disease.
3   Asthma is caused by a germ.
4   Meningitis can easily be spread in an overcrowded place.
5   Malaria is a disease caused by an allergy.
6   Tuberculosis can be prevented by a vaccine.
7   Improved personal and public hygiene can prevent cholera.
8   A high body temperature could be a sign of a disease.

Activity set 2

Children's clinic card

Objective

When we come to the end of this section you should be able to:
*   describe and spot the differences between blank and used children's clinic cards.

Activities

1   On the blank children's clinic card, study the following things carefully:
   a)   section on child's family information.
   b)   section on immunisation.
   c)   section showing weight/age graph.
   d)   some information about foods.
   ?   What information should be put on the section concerning the child's family?
2   Examine the immunisation programme part.
   ?   Which disease should the child be immunised against first?
   ?   What do the horizontal lines show on the graph?
   ?   What do the vertical lines show?
   ?   What do the diagonal lines show?

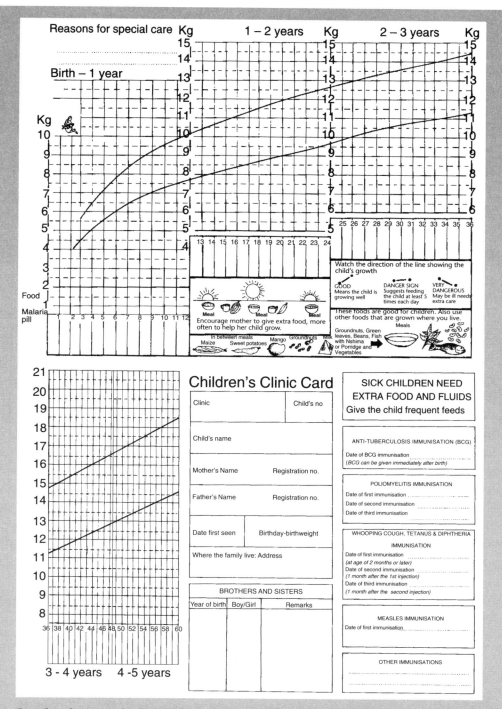

3 Study the used children's clinic cards which you brought with you.
- What is the average weight of a child who is 10 months old?
- Which diseases are the children immunised against?

3   Using the measuring strip of paper prepared by your teacher, measure around the mid-arm of a five year old child.
  ☐   What is the length of the strip of paper that has gone round the arm?
  ☐   Has the length reached the red, yellow or green mark?
  ☐   What does this show?

Information

When germs get into a person's body, they quickly multiply. They make poisons in the body. These poisons are signs of sickness referred to as symptoms.

The blood system brings special cells to the infected part of the body and begin to fight the disease. These special cells are called **white blood cells**.

If the infection is on the skin where you can see it, you will also be able to see a yellow substance called **pus.**

Pus consists of germs that have been killed by white blood cells. As a person recovers from the disease, other white blood cells produce **antibodies**. Antibodies are chemicals that remain in the blood to fight germs of a particular disease. The disease's symptoms disappear and the person is said to be **immunised** against that disease. If germs which cause the same disease are introduced into the immunised person, he/she may be able to fight that disease.

When a person is **immune** to a disease, the antibodies for that disease are already in the blood stream. There are two ways of becoming immunised. One way is that the body can become immunised by getting the disease and then making its own antibodies. The other way is by injecting dead germs into the body. The body then makes antibodies to fight those dead germs.

The diagram below shows the defence system of the body using white blood cells and antibodies to fight germs and viruses.

Fig. 6.1.3 Defence mechanisms

Vaccine is the word used for the liquid which destroys the germs which cause diseases. The process of giving people **vaccinations** against diseases is known as **immunisation**.

At the front of a child's clinic card, there is information about immunisation. There are six different diseases written on it, which children should be immunised against. These are diseases which children can get very easily. These diseases can kill children if they are not immunised against them.

Age	Immunisation
At birth	Anti-Tuberculosis (BCG)
At 2 months or later	Diptheria, Pertussis (whooping cough) Tetanus (commonly known as DPT) and Poliomyelitis
At 9 months	Measles
At 3 months and at 4 months (or later)	Booster for DPT and poliomyelitis
At primary school entry age (5-6 yrs)	Booster BCG
At primary school learning age (7-9yrs)	Booster BCG

In addition to the immunisation programme, the clinic card contains a weight and age graph to help check whether the child is growing normally or not. The child's date of birth is shown on the card too.

Another way of monitoring a child's growth is by measuring the child's arm circumference. A healthy child's arm circumference increases by just a little more than 1 cm between its first birthday and its fifth birthday. By five years of age, the arm circumference of a healthy child should be between 16 cm and 17 cm. If it is less, the child is malnourished.

Fig. 6.1.4 Mid-arm circumference

The strip has different colours on it to show whether the child's arm has a healthy circumference or not. The colours are:

Red for danger — the child's arm is too small, therefore the child could be malnourished.

Yellow for warning — the child's arm is small, but not too small, meaning that the child is getting proper food but could do with even more better food.

Green for good — the child's arm is a healthy size, meaning that the child is getting enough good food.

Fig. 6.1.5 Health centre

 Written exercise 6.2

1   The time line on page 77 is marked in years, from birth to 14 years of age. Three points are marked on the time line. They are shown by thick lines and labelled A, B and C. Use the immunisation programme

chart to write down which vaccinations children should be given at the ages marked: **A**, **B** and **C**.

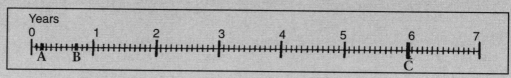

2   Choose the correct words from those given in the list below to complete the blank spaces in the passage. Write the complete passage in your exercise book.

antibodies, vaccination, immunised, injection, germs, symptoms

People who are _____ against a disease can come into contact with the germs that cause the disease without getting any _____. A person can become immune to a disease once he/she has suffered from it or as a result of _____. Nowadays, children are vaccinated to make them immune to some dangerous diseases.

   When a person is vaccinated, weakened or dead _____ are put into the body. This is usually done by an _____. The body makes _____. These will attack similar germs and make them harmless. Once the body has made antibodies against a disease, the person is protected from that disease if he/she comes into contact with the germs which cause the disease.

3   Using the measuring strips of paper prepared by your teacher, measure around the mid-arm of a five-year old child.
   a)   What is the length of the strip that has gone round the arm?
   b)   Has the length reached the red, yellow or green mark?
   c)   What does this show?

Activity Set 3

Rapid population growth and health

Objectives

By the end of this section you should be able to:
*   describe the effects of diseases on human population.
*   identify consequences of rapid population growth on health facilities.

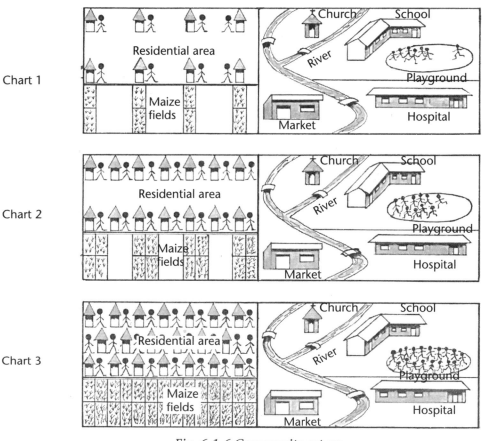

Chart 1

Chart 2

Chart 3

Fig. 6.1.6 Community set up

Activities

1   In groups of four, study Chart 1 and discuss the community. Looking
    at the number of people, houses and the space left between houses,
    ⍰   do people have enough space around their homes? Why?
2   Study Chart 2.
    ⍰   Why are more houses built in the community?
    ⍰   What caused the population to grow?
3   Study Chart 3.
    ⍰   Can you say that this community has grown too quickly? Why?
    ⍰   What diseases are people in Charts 2 and 3 likely to suffer from?
    ⍰   Why?
    ⍰   How is the Government going to be affected by the rapid growth
        of communities 2 and 3?

Information

When a population grows rapidly, epidemics like cholera, dysentry and meningitis can take place. This may result in a number of people losing their lives. This would reduce the productive capacity of the nation in many ways. Rapid growth affects health care systems as well. This is because the normal services rendered become inadequate. For example, it becomes expensive to provide more trained personnel to meet the health needs of a growing population.

In a rapid growing nation, mothers of reproductive age and children under five years of age are at the highest risk of diseases and death. These two groups of people would require more medical attention than other groups in the population. Rapid growth puts pressure on health personnel, such as doctors and nurses. When the number of doctors and nurses per given population reduces, many patients can be seriously affected. This makes it necessary for the ratio of doctors to population to be maintained at a higher level.

World Health Organisation (WHO) recommends a minimum of one doctor per 10 000 people. Most developing countries fail to meet this minimum ratio. Zambia, for example, in 1988 had a ratio of 0.67 doctors per 10 000 people. This low ratio was a result of a high rate of population growth, or fertility rate, compared to the supply rate of medical personnel.

✎ Written exercise 6.3

Fill in the missing words in the following passage by using words listed below the passage.

Rapid _____ growth affects _____ care delivery systems. The services delivered when there is a _____ population growth are not _____ . High _____ rate which is the main factor leading to a rapid population growth, determines the number of high health risk persons in a _____ .

expensive	community	population
enough	health	fertility
rapid	doctors	patients

Activity set 4

HIV/AIDS

Objectives

When you come to the end of this section you should be able to:
*   describe what HIV/AIDS is.
*   discuss, with understanding, ways in which HIV/AIDS can be spread.

HIV: Human Immuno-Deficiency Virus
AIDS: Acquired Immune Deficiency Syndrome

Activities

1   Study the following picture.

Fig. 6.1.7 Persons at a bus stop

⏺   Which people do you think have HIV/AIDS? Why?
⏺   Can you tell that a person has HIV/AIDS by merely looking at them?
2   If you are told that the person sitting next to you has the HIV virus,
     what would you do if he/she did the following:
⏺   hands you a piece of bread that he has been eating?
⏺   asks you to shake hands?

 [?]   asks you to kiss?
 [?]   asks you to use the same tooth brush that he has used?
 [?]   requests you to wash his/her clothes?
 [?]   asks you to visit his/her home?
 [?]   asks you to use the same razor blade to cut your nails?

3   Banda has been found not to have enough blood in his body by medical doctors. Discuss ways in which he can have his blood increased.

Information

HIV stands for Human Immuno-Deficiency Virus. The HIV virus, unlike other viruses, enters the body and destroys those cells that are responsible for defending the body against other diseases such as diarrhoea, tuberculosis, coughs and many others. The state of having the HIV virus is known as being **HIV positive** while the absence of the HIV virus in the body is called **HIV negative**.

Caution
*An HIV positive person can only be identified by carrying out an **HIV test**.*

AIDS stands for Acquired Immune Deficiency Syndrome.
Acquired: getting from somebody
Immune: the body's defensive system
Defficiency: lacking/inability to fight infection
Syndrome: several ways in which the disease shows itself

When one has AIDS, the natural body protection system (the Human Immune System) is weakened. The **immune system** is the means by which the body protects itself from infection and disease. It consists mainly of the white blood cells which deal with harmful organisms such as bacteria and viruses.

AIDS is spread largely through sexual contact with people infected with the HIV virus. Apart from sexual contact, the HIV virus can be passed from one person to another through blood, for example, from a mother with the HIV virus to her child before or at birth.

Blood transfusion is another way through which the HIV virus can be spread. Since the HIV virus lives in the blood, it can be transmitted by the transfusion of blood from an infected blood donor to an uninfected person. HIV can also be transmitted through the use of syringes, needles, knives, blades, surgical instruments and other piercing instruments that have been used on an infected person and not sterilised properly. This also includes instruments used for circumcision, tattooing, acupuncture, ear piercing and intravenous drugs. The transmission of the HIV virus is also made easier by the presence of other STDs (Sexually Transmitted Diseases) such as gonorrhea and syphillis. If one has an STD, the risk of being infected by the HIV virus during sexual intercourse with an infected person is very high. This is so because the sores will provide an opening through which the virus will enter. Due to the loss of the body's ability to defend itself against certain diseases, the following will show:

1 prolonged cough
2 fever and night sweats
3 unexplained weight loss
4 prolonged diarrhoea
5 enlarged glands mainly in the neck and armpits
6 itchy and painful skin rashes
7 herpes zoster
8 *carposis sacoma*
9 tuberculosis

These are not necessarily the results of HIV infection and it is therefore important to go to the hospital to be examined and be tested for HIV/AIDS before you conclude that one has the HIV virus or AIDS.

 Written exercise 6.4

Write down *true* or *false* for these statements about HIV/AIDS.
1 You can get HIV/AIDS by just sitting next to an infected person.
2 Mosquito bites can spread HIV/AIDS.
3 HIV is not transmitted by shaking hands.
4 Some traditional healers can cure AIDS.
5 Some people may have HIV or STD and might not know it.
6 AIDS damages the body's immune system.
7 AIDS is a number of diseases that invade the body.
8 STDs are diseases that are transmitted through sexual intercourse.

Activity set 5

Prevention of HIV/AIDS

Objective

By the end of this section you should be able to:
*   discuss how HIV/AIDS can be prevented.

Fig. 6.1.8 Spread of HIV

Activities

1   Study the picture above in groups, and answer the following questions:
    ❓   What are the people in the picture doing?
    ❓   By looking at the position in which they appear to be, is it easy to say no to sexual intercourse?

> [?]   Is it good for a man and woman to be alone in a room for too long?
> [?]   What may happen if one accepted gifts and money from people especially of the opposite sex who are not known to them or trusted?
> [?]   What would accepting free rides in the cars from people you do not know or trust do to you?
> [?]   When is the right time to use a condom?
> [?]   How is it used?
> [?]   Should married people also use condoms?
> (Your teacher will show you condoms and help you understand how they are used, why they are used and when.)

Information

AIDS was first identified in Zambia in 1981 and since then, many people have died from the epidemic. It has been reported in many parts of the world and to date it has no cure or vaccine.

There are several ways of preventing HIV infection. These include:
— sticking to one faithful partner.
— not having sex until the right time when one is ready.
— having protected sex, for example, using condoms.
— avoiding pregnancies when infected with HIV.

 Written exercise 6.5

Write *true* or *false* for the following statements.
1   Young people should realise that if they do not protect themselves, they could get HIV infection.
2   It is all right to have sexual intercourse without a condom, because the chance of getting HIV infection is very low.
3   It is safer not to have sexual intercourse as a teenager.
4   If people think they might have sexual intercourse they should carry a condom with them.
5   Young people can inject drugs once in a while without the risk of getting HIV infection.
6   It would be all right to be in the same room with someone who has AIDS.

Chapter

7

ENERGY

Forms of energy

Objective

By the end of this section you should be able to:
* identify various forms of energy and their sources.

Activities

1 In pairs, tell each other some of the things you do from the time you wake up in the morning to the time you go to bed in the evening.
   ? Do you know why you do these things?
   ? For example, do you know why you eat food?
   ? What would happen if you had no food for the whole day?
   ? What does food do to your body?
2 Study the pictures below.

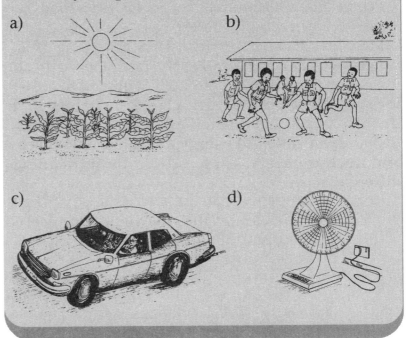

a)

b)

c)

d)

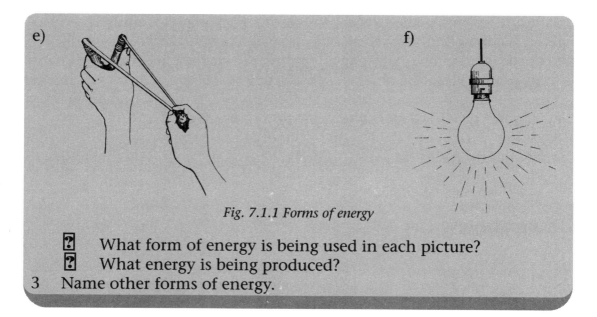

Fig. 7.1.1 Forms of energy

?   What form of energy is being used in each picture?
?   What energy is being produced?
3   Name other forms of energy.

Information

People do a lot of activities such as running, jumping, climbing, playing football, working, driving and others. In all these activities **energy** is needed. Where do people get this energy from? It is not only people who do work. Other things such as animals, machines, wind and water also do **work**.

People and other animals get energy from food. Food is our fuel. It burns inside us and gives off energy.

Machines also need energy. They get energy from fuels. For example, a car gets energy from petrol in the tank. On earth, almost all the energy we use comes from the sun. Sunlight is needed to grow the food. The fuels we use such as coal, petrol, gas and oil were formed millions of years ago with the help of the sun. Energy exists in various forms. The forms of energy include **heat** and **light energy, chemical energy, electrical energy, sound and nuclear energy. These various forms of energy are produced from different sources.**

Heat and light energy are produced directly from the sun. They can also be produced from burning fuels like wood. Electrical energy can be produced with the help of burning fuels. It can also be produced with the help of water at hydroelectric power stations. This is one of the most useful types of energy. Chemical energy is stored in food, fuels and cells. It is also used in radios, torches and watches. Kinetic energy is produced by moving objects. The faster an object moves the more kinetic energy it has. This energy is sometimes called **moving energy.**

Potential energy is the energy that is stored by objects waiting to be used later. It is stored in non-moving objects such as a stretched catapult, springs and elastic bands. Potential energy is often called **stored energy.** Sound energy is produced by vibrating objects such as a guitar, a banjo, a drum and radios.

One of the most recently discovered forms of energy is **nuclear energy.** Nuclear energy comes from the explosion of **atoms**.

Looking at the described forms of energy above, we can now say that energy makes things do work or move. Therefore, energy is the ability to get things moving or done.

✎ Written exercise 7.1

1   Match the pictures with the appropriate form of energy.

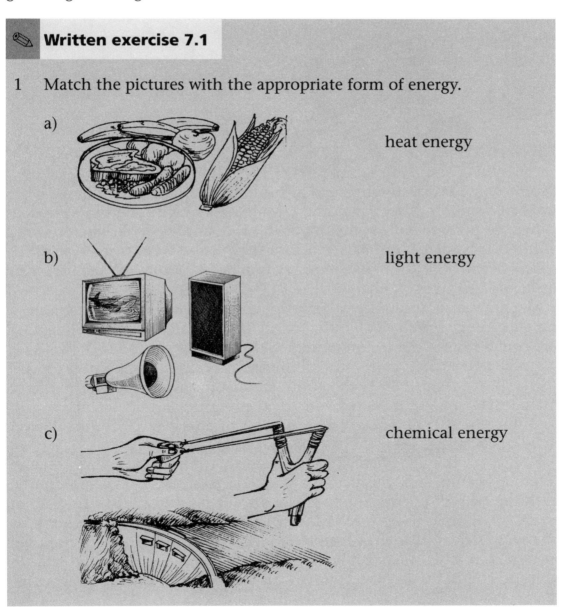

a)   heat energy

b)   light energy

c)   chemical energy

d) 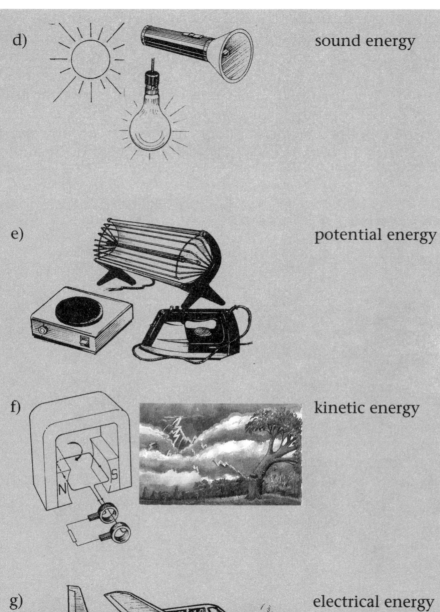 sound energy

e) potential energy

f) kinetic energy

g) electrical energy

Fig. 7.1.2 Forms of energy

Activity Set 2

Energy changes

Objective

By the end of this section pupils will be able to:
*   describe how energy changes from one form to the other.

1   Study the pictures below.

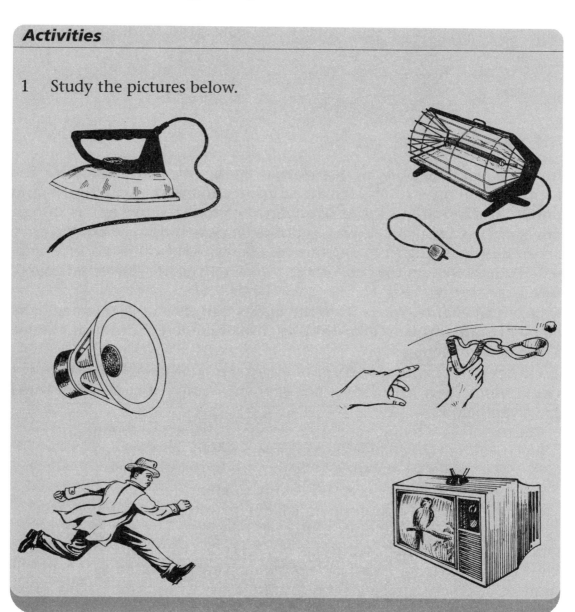

Fig. 7.1.3 Energy transformations

The machines above are able to change or convert one form of energy to the other. In pairs, discuss the changes that take place each time.
2   Name other things that work by changing one form of energy to the other.
3   Electrical energy can be changed into many forms of energy. Name some of them.

Information

In the previous lesson, we learnt that energy has various forms. The forms of energy are **electrical**, **sound**, **chemical**, **heat**, **light** and **potential**. The various forms of energy are produced by various things. Energy is used whenever work is done. When things use energy, they are simply changing from one form of energy to the other. For example, when you switch on the cooker, the cooker will change electrical energy into heat energy.

Electrical energy comes from the mains into the cooker element, the element **transforms** or changes this electrical energy into heat energy. The element becomes hot.

Things that change one form of energy to another are called **energy converters**. There are many kinds of energy converters. Some of them are given below:

Car battery — changes chemical energy to electrical energy.
Electrical bulb — changes electrical energy to light energy.
Heater — changes electrical energy to heat energy.
Catapult — changes potential energy to kinetic energy.
Human beings — change chemical energy into kinetic energy.
Chemical energy comes from the food we eat.
One of the commonly used forms of energy is **electrical energy** simply known as **electricity.** It can be used along wires and taken to where it is needed. Electrical energy can be converted or changed into many other forms of energy. We can change electrical energy into light energy in radios

or television sets. This energy, though widely used, is also expensive. We must conserve it.

✎ Written exercise 7.2

Complete these sentences.
1   A car battery changes _____ energy into _____ energy.
2   A telephone set changes _____ energy into electrical energy and back into _____ energy.
3   An athlete changes _____ energy into _____ energy.
4   A bulb changes _____ energy into _____ and heat energy.
5   A car changes _____ energy into _____ energy.

Activity Set 3

The hydroelectric power station

Objective

By the end of this section you should be able to:
*   describe the energy changes taking place at a hydroelectric power station.

Activities

1   In groups, discuss how electricity is produced at a hydropower station and explain the energy changes that take place.
2   Study the diagram of the hydropower station below.

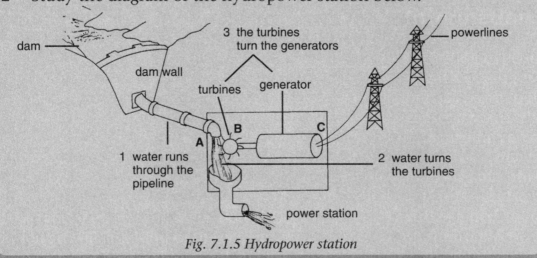

Fig. 7.1.5 Hydropower station

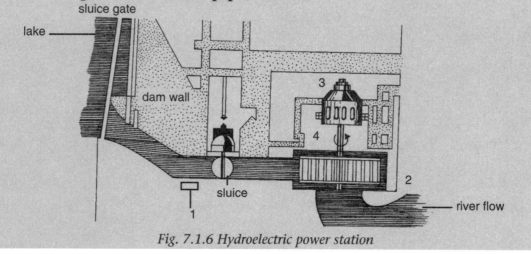

What energy changes take place at A?
What energy changes take place at B?
What energy changes take place at C?

Information

Most of the electrical energy we use in our homes comes from hydropower stations. In Zambia the big hydroelectric power stations include Kariba and Itedzi tedzi. At these power stations, electricity is produced from water powered generators. The process of making electricity starts from the dam. The stored water behind a dam has potential energy. When water is allowed to run down into pipes, it converts potential energy into kinetic energy. The water goes to turn huge motors called **water turbines**. The kinetic energy from water is converted into mechanical energy when turbines start to turn.

The turbines turn generators and the generators produce the **electrical energy** commonly known as **electricity**. The electricity produced by hydroelectric power stations is very high but it is reduced to between 220 V to 240 V by **transformers**. Our homes usually use 220 V to 240 V of mains electricity.

✎ Written exercise 7.3

1   Write the energy change for the model water wheel.
2   Here is a drawing of a real hydroelectric power station. Four important parts are numbered. Choose the correct names of the numbered parts from the list. Write the numbers and correct names in your exercise book.

shaft, generator, water pipe, turbine

Fig. 7.1.6 Hydroelectric power station

Activity Set 4

Wind energy

Objective

By the end of this section you should be able to:
*   describe how wind energy can be used.

Activities

1   Follow the instructions on how to make a windmill.
    Use a piece of manila paper of about 15 cm by 15 cm. Divide the
    paper into four parts as shown below.

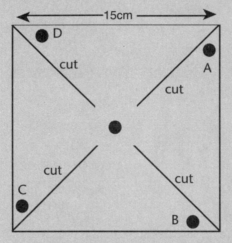

2   Cut out the parts A and C and make a hole in the centre as shown below.
3   Use a small piece of grass and push it through a maize stalk as shown.

(i) 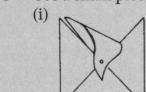   (ii) 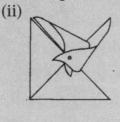   (iii)   (iv)

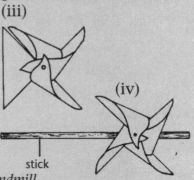

stick

Fig. 7.1.7 How to make a windmill

2   Fix your windmill to the maize stalk using the piece of grass. Direct the windmill towards the direction where the wind is coming from.
    ❓   What happens?
    ❓   Discuss how you can use the windmill in other ways.
3   Study the picture below:
    ❓   How is the windmill in the picture used?
    ❓   Where have you seen a windmill in Zambia?
    ❓   Can it be used for other things?
    ❓   What happens when the wind stops blowing?
4   Suggest other ways the windmill can be used.

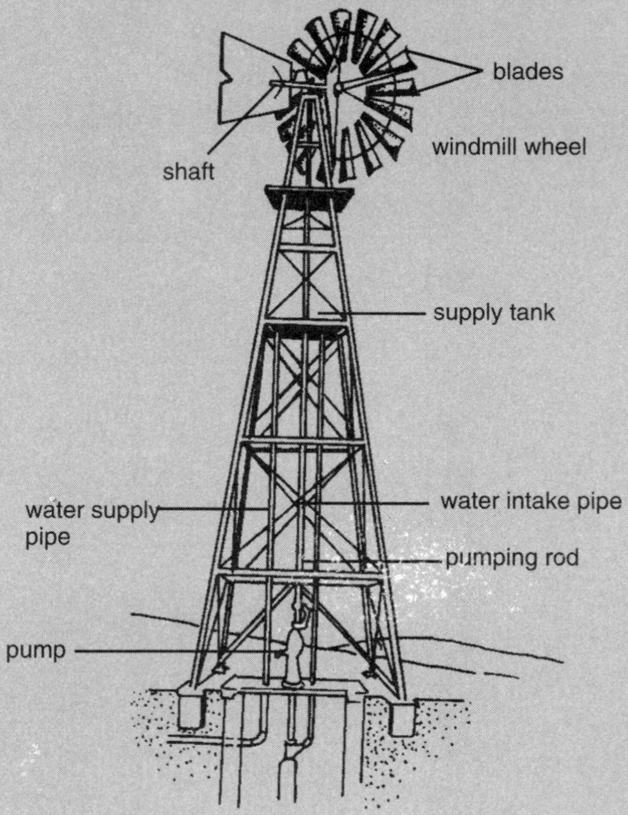

Fig. 7.1.8 Windmill

Information

Have you ever tried to find out about the type of energy you use at home? Do you know how much it costs and how long it will last. Most of the energy we use in our homes/industries comes from fuels like firewood, coal, oil and gas.

Some of these fuels are expensive to obtain and they do not last forever.

Scientists are working hard to find other sources of energy which will be cheaper and long lasting. Some of these are **solar energy** which comes from the sun. Although the sun's energy comes to us free, the solar panels or cells are expensive to make. The other cheaper source of energy is energy from the wind. The energy from the wind can be used by connecting windmills which generators use to produce electricity. In Zambia, windmills are used to pump water.

Although wind energy is cheaper, it has one disadvantage. It can only be used when the the wind is blowing.

 Written exercise 7.4

1   Name the possible situations where people make use of wind energy.
2   Write the energy chain for the steps in the working windmill.
3   What do we call energy from the sun?

Chapter 8

ECOLOGY

Activity Set 1

Food chains and food webs

Objective

By the end of this chapter you should be able to:
- identify producers, consumers and decomposers in a food chain or food web.

Activities

1   Check around the school for small animals or insects. Observe what they are eating. Look for creatures such as bees, locusts, birds, lizards, chameleons, caterpillars, snakes and others.
2   In groups, discuss what these animals eat.
3   Put the animals into two groups. One group should be for those that eat plants and another one for those that eat other animals.
4   In groups, discuss what happens to things when they die. For example:
   ❓   What happens to the plants in the compost heap?
   ❓   How about dead animals?

Information

All living things have to feed in order to stay alive. Living things include plants, animals and bacteria. Plants make their own food using energy from the sun. Animals feed on plants and other animals. Bacteria feed on dead animals and decaying material.

Most living things on earth depend on plants for their food. Plants are known as **producers** of food.

Animals that feed on plants are known as **consumers**, while bacteria are known as **decomposers**. We can say that producers are eaten by consumers while both producers and consumers are fed on by decomposers.

A chain showing how living things depend on each other is called a **food chain**, for example, a plant is eaten by a caterpillar and a caterpillar is eaten by a bird. This can be written in a food chain as follows:

Leaves → **caterpillar** → **bird.**

A number of food chains linked together is called a **food web.**

 Written exercise 8.1

1   Write down four examples of consumers.
2   Name the animals known as decomposers.
3   Which living things are known as consumers?
4   Make a food chain for each of the following list of living things.
 a)   man, worm, chicken
 b)   lion, rabbit, grass
 c)   mosquito, gecko, snake
 d)   toad, snake, worm

Activity Set 2

The rain cycle

Objective

By the end of this section you should be able to:
*   describe the rain cycle.

Activities

1   In groups, discuss how rain is formed.
 ?   Where do clouds come from?
 ?   What makes rain fall?
2   Look at the picture on page 98 showing the rain cycle and answer the questions that follow:

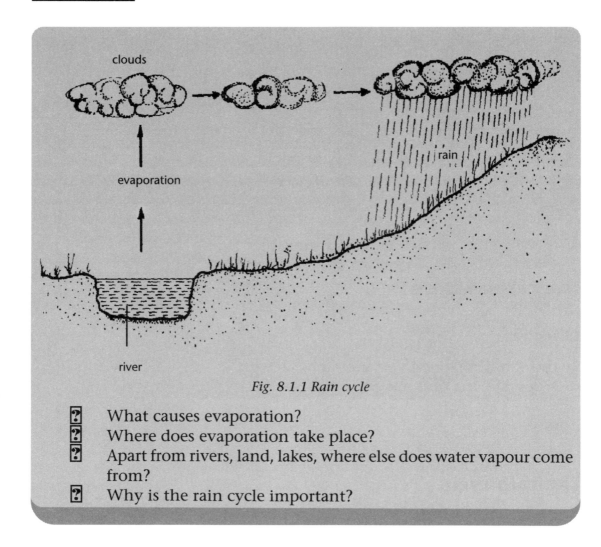

Fig. 8.1.1 Rain cycle

[?] What causes evaporation?
[?] Where does evaporation take place?
[?] Apart from rivers, land, lakes, where else does water vapour come from?
[?] Why is the rain cycle important?

Information

Almost all the water we use on earth comes from rain. The water comes to us through a process called the **rain cycle**. The rain cycle is part of the natural water system on earth. For the rain to fall, a process has to take place. For example, water from rivers and oceans is heated first. It starts to evaporate. When this water vapour reaches the cold space high up, it changes into tiny drops of water. These drops of water join together to form clouds. When more and more drops of water collect on the clouds, they start to fall as rain.

When the rain falls, the water collects in rivers and oceans. The process of evaporation starts once more. This process goes on and on. This is why it is called the **rain cycle**.

✎ Written exercise 8.2

Use the words below to fill in the blanks.
oceans, evaporation, rain cycle, rain, lakes, condensation
1   The natural water system on earth is known as_____.
2   The changing of water vapour into droplets is known as _____ .
3   The rising of water vapour is called _____ .
4   Evaporation takes place mainly from ——— and ——— .
5   Almost all the water on earth comes from _____ .

Activity Set 3

The carbon cycle

Objective

By the end this section you should be able to:
•   describe the carbon cycle.

Activities

1   In groups discuss the air animals use for breathing.
   ?   What air is breathed out?
   ?   Where does most air we use come from?
   ?   What air do plants use?
2   Light a candle. Place a glass jar carefully over the lit candle. Observe what happens.

Information

Most of the air we breathe out is carbon dioxide. Other sources of carbon dioxide in the atmosphere are decomposing plants and burning of things, such as oil, gas and coal. We can actually know that the gas is carbon dioxide when it puts out fire.

Carbon dioxide is also removed from the atmosphere by plants. During photosynthesis, plants use energy from the sun and carbon dioxide from the atmosphere to make food.

The whole process can be written as a **cycle**.

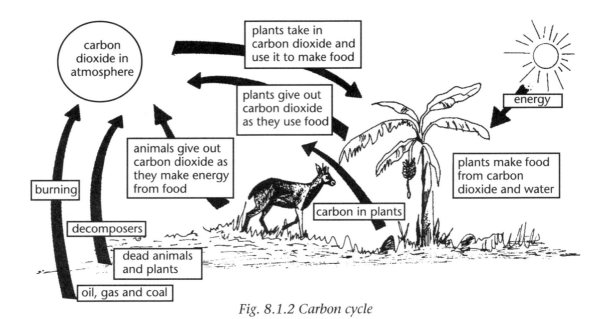

Fig. 8.1.2 Carbon cycle

Carbon dioxide is used in fire extinguishers and other fire fighting equipment because it does not support burning.

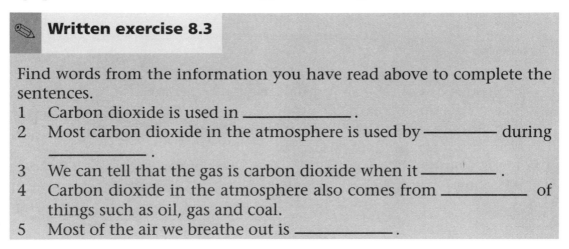

Written exercise 8.3

Find words from the information you have read above to complete the sentences.

1   Carbon dioxide is used in ——————— .
2   Most carbon dioxide in the atmosphere is used by ——————— during ——————— .
3   We can tell that the gas is carbon dioxide when it ——————— .
4   Carbon dioxide in the atmosphere also comes from ——————— of things such as oil, gas and coal.
5   Most of the air we breathe out is ——————— .

Activity Set 4

The nitrogen cycle

Objectives

By the end of this section you should be able to:
•   describe the nitrogen cycle.
•   describe the effect of less nitrogen on plants.

Activities

1   Find a young tomato plant. Pull it out of the soil carefully. Wash the soil off the roots. Stand the plant in a jar of water. Add either red or blue dye in the water. Leave this for some hours. Observe what happens after one or two hours.

2   After two hours, record what you can see on the stem and leaves of the plant. Remove the plant from the water. Cut across the stem and study it carefully.

    ▷   What do you see in the stem?

    ?   How did the ink you see get in the stem?

3   Discuss with your friends why we water our gardens.

    ?   What happens if we stopped watering the gardens?

Information

Plants make their own food by using energy from the sun and carbon dioxide from the atmosphere. Apart from these, the plant also gets nutrients from the soil. One of these nutrients is **nitrogen**. The plants get nitrogen from the soil through the roots.

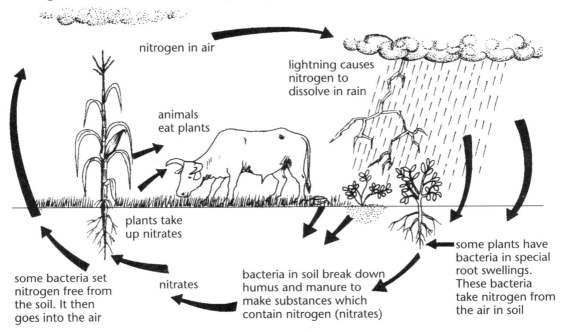

Fig. 8.1.2 Nitrogen cycle

In the atmosphere, nitrogen gas forms the biggest part of the air. But nitrogen has to go into the soil in order to be taken by plants. The continuous supply of nitrogen depends on the food chains and food webs. This process is called the **nitrogen cycle**.

The nitrogen cycle starts from when animals and plants die. Their remains rot or decompose as a result of bacteria in the soil. During decomposition, some nitrogen from plants and animals remain in the soil.

Plants get this nitrogen from the soil. Animals also eat or feed on these plants. When these animals and plants die, nitrogen remains in the soil and the cycle goes on. Farmers also help to increase nitrogen in the soil by the use of fertilisers.

Written exercise 8.4

Copy and complete the nitrogen cycle in your book.

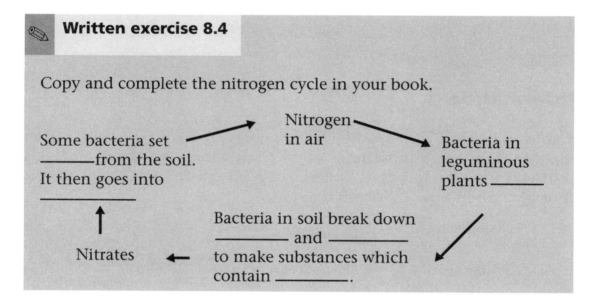

Activity Set 5

Crop rotation

Objective

By the end of this section you should be able to:
* describe crop rotation.

Activities

1   Look at the crops in your garden.

? Do they look healthy? Why?
? What crops have been grown in your school garden?
? How long have such crops been grown?
? Have you been growing the same crop throughout ? Why?
? Have the crops been healthy? Why?

Information

Planting the same crop throughout the year makes the soil unhealthy. The crops grown in that piece of land become unhealthy.

Plant nutrients in that soil become used up by the crop so much that later, crops grown will not have enough nutrients. A method know as **crop rotation** should be practised. Crop rotation helps to bring back some nutrients into the soil.

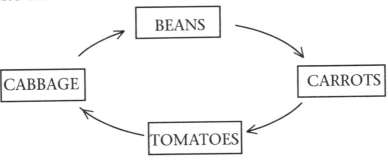

Fig 8.1.3 Crop rotation

Crops like groundnuts and beans bring back nutrients into the soil. Such crops either have to be grown side by side with other crops or rotated with such crops.

Crop rotation helps to prevent pests and diseases.

Some farmers practise a method called **fallowing**. This is when the land is left bare for a certain period before other crops are grown again.

✎ **Written exercise 8.5**

1   Use this table to record your example of soil losing its fertility and your ideas on how to solve these problems.

Way of losing soil fertility	How to solve the problem

2   This plan shows a crop rotation system for three plots over a four year period. Answer the questions below.

Year → Plot ↓	1	2	3	4
1	maize			
2	groundnuts			
3	cassava			

a)   Which crop is to be grown in plot 3 in year 4?
b)   Which crop can be grown in the same plot two years in a row, if necessary?
c)   Which crop is to be grown in plot 4 in year 1?

Activity Set 6

The balance in nature

Objective

By the end of this section you should be able to:
•   describe how the balance in nature can be disturbed and how it affects human life.

Activities

1   Study the picture below.

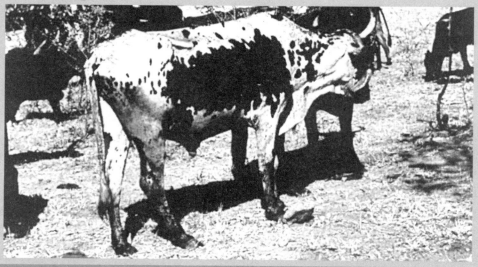

?   Why are the animals looking the way they do?
?   How could that have been stopped?
2   Choose a piece of land near your school and study all the animals on it.
3   Discuss in groups what would happen if all the grass was removed.
4   Look at the fish pond.
    ?   What do you find living in that environment?
    ?   What would happen if you removed plants in the fish pond?
    ?   Why?

Information

Living things depend on one another for food. This is called a **balance in nature**. If part of the environment is disturbed, life of the animals in that type of environment is endangered. Animals and plants will die. An example is the destruction of all grass. All the animals that depend on the grass would die because they would have no food to eat. Those animals that depend on those that eat grass will also die.

The interdependence of animals can be shown by a food chain. For example;

$$\text{grass} \xrightarrow[\text{by}]{\text{eaten}} \text{impala} \xrightarrow[\text{by}]{\text{eaten}} \text{lion}$$

Written exercise 8.6

1   Draw a diagram showing two animals that depend on grass.
2   Draw another diagram to show what would happen to the animals if all the plants were removed.
3   Draw a food chain of living things in a fish pond.

Activity Set 7

Soil erosion and overgrazing

Objective

By the end of this section you should be able to:
*   discuss the effects of overgrazing.

Activities

1   Visit your school garden.
    ▷   Observe the soil in it.
        Feel the soil.
2   Go to another area where there is no grass or trees. Feel the soil.
    ❓   What is the difference?
3   Look at the picture below:

Fig. 8.1.4 Bare ground

❓   What happened to the grass in the picture?
❓   What might happen to the soil in the picture?

Information

Land which is constantly grazed by animals such as goats, cows, impala and other animals may have its soil eroded. The animals may eat all the grass and leave the land bare. This is what causes **soil erosion**. Soil erosion is the washing away of top soil by either wind, or fast moving water. Overgrazing by animals causes soil erosion. Their hooves tramp on the soil and make it loose so that when wind blows, the soil is carried away. Fast moving water from rain or rivers also carries away the loose top soil.

✏ Written exercise 8.7

Fill in the missing words.
1 The carrying away of top soil by wind or water is called —————.
2 ————— causes soil erosion.
3 The ————— of animals make the soil —————.